From Babel to Zarahemla

A Journey of Faith and Divine Guidance

Cooper Neitzel

Library of Congress Control Number: 2024924504

Published by Hemingway Publishers

Cover design by Hemingway Publishers

ISBN: Printed in the United States

Table of Contents

General Description

From Babel to Zarahemla: A Journey of Faith and Divine Guidance *is the first volume of the* Promised Land *series, inviting readers to undertake a rich spiritual expedition—from the confusion of Babel to the promised land of Zarahemla.*

This final book is more than a retelling of the Jaredite journey between around 2000 BCE and around 200 BCE. It is an exploration of universal spiritual truths woven through the lens of world religions to reveal an extraordinary tapestry of faith, resilience, and divine guidance.

At the heart of this journey lies the Book of Ether, one of the most profound narratives in the Book of Mormon. The Jaredite story becomes more than ancient history—it emerges as a metaphor for the universal quest for meaning, purpose, and spiritual fulfillment. From Babel's scattering of language to the enlightenment and peace found in Zarahemla, this journey crosses ages and cultures, speaking to a universal human experience. As we trace the paths of Jared, the brother of Jared, and their people, we uncover timeless lessons on prayer, humility, repentance, and the strength required to overcome adversity.

The story is enriched with perspectives from major world religions—Judaism, Christianity, Islam, Hinduism, Buddhism, and the teachings of The Church of Jesus Christ of Latter-day Saints. Each faith tradition brings to light shared spiritual principles that transcend borders and beliefs, guiding readers toward a personal "promised land." Here, themes such as faith, humility, repentance, and moral integrity come alive, demonstrating that these principles are universal roadmaps for a life well-lived.

From Babel to Zarahemla invites readers to see the Jaredite story as a mirror of their own journey. The book poses questions that have resonated throughout human history: How do we find divine guidance in a world filled with distractions? How do we build faith that endures life's "great deeps"? And, ultimately, how do we reach our own spiritual "promised lands," places of peace and divine connection? By interweaving scripture with insights from global spiritual traditions, this book helps readers find tools to strengthen their faith, deepen their understanding of divine guidance, and pursue a life aligned with enduring spiritual values.

Whether you are a student of scripture, a seeker of wisdom, or someone navigating the uncertainties of life, *From Babel to Zarahemla* will enrich your understanding of what it means to walk a path of faith, resilience, and humility. In this journey, Zarahemla is more than a physical destination—it is a spiritual state, a place of inner peace and profound connection to God, waiting to be discovered by each soul willing to embark on the journey.

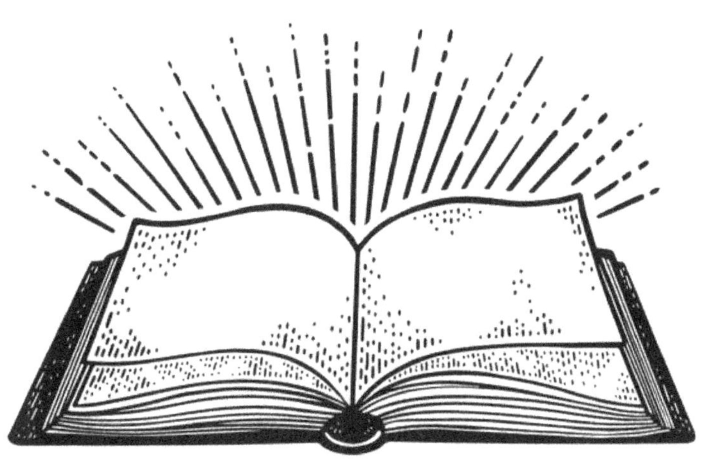

Introduction: Babel and Zarahemla— From Origin to Destination

Babel as the Spiritual Origin of the Journey

Babel stands as a monumental starting point, where human ambition, pride, and divine intervention collide, creating a landscape rich with spiritual lessons and symbolic depth. Historically, Babel is the site where humanity sought to elevate itself—quite literally—to the heavens. In the pursuit of unity and greatness, the people of Babel embarked on an ambitious project: to construct a tower that would touch the sky, a symbol of their determination to overcome earthly limits and establish a name for themselves. But what started as a communal endeavor soon crossed into the realm of hubris, prompting divine intervention that would change the course of human history and set the stage for our own spiritual journey.

In the sacred texts of Judaism, Christianity, and Islam, Babel is more than just an ancient city; it is a powerful metaphor. In the Jewish tradition, the story of Babel serves as a cautionary tale about the dangers of prideful unity that lacks reverence for divine authority. The Midrash portrays Babel's builders as driven not by devotion but by a desire to defy divine order, seeking to control their own destiny rather than humbly accept the guidance of God. This narrative underscores the importance of humility and the wisdom of respecting divine boundaries, warning that unity without a higher purpose can lead to confusion rather than harmony.

In Christianity, Babel takes on similar themes of ambition and humility. The New Testament echoes these lessons, warning against the arrogance that blinds people to their reliance on God. Babel becomes a symbol of human fallibility, a reminder that the journey toward spiritual understanding requires the dissolution of pride. Christians are taught that divine guidance comes when one's heart is turned toward God rather than self-elevation, transforming the scattering at Babel into an invitation to seek unity not solely through human achievement but through divine love.

In Islam, the story of Babel emphasizes the wisdom and mercy in God's intervention. The Quran acknowledges human diversity as a purposeful act of divine creation, a way to encourage understanding and collaboration among different peoples. For Muslims, Babel represents the limits of human ambition when it stands in contrast to submission to Allah. The scattering of languages is not merely punishment but a call to humility and faith, a reminder that true greatness lies not in defying God's will but in embracing it. Babel's legacy is one of humility before the Creator, illustrating the beauty of diversity as a sign of divine wisdom rather than division.

From these rich traditions, Babel emerges as the spiritual origin of our journey—a place of dissonance that calls us toward harmony, of confusion that invites us to seek divine clarity. The scattering of languages and cultures becomes a symbol of spiritual fragmentation, one that can only be resolved by turning back to the divine. Babel reminds us that while human ambition is not inherently wrong, it must be rooted in humility and guided by a higher purpose. The journey from Babel to Zarahemla, then, is a journey from the chaos of pride and self-reliance to the peace and unity found in divine guidance.

As Elder D. Todd Christofferson observed, "Trying to find a different course to heaven is like the futility of working on the Tower of Babel rather than looking to Christ and His salvation." Babel reminds us of the spiritual dead-ends we encounter when we attempt to chart our own course, ignoring the guidance of divine light. In contrast, Zarahemla represents a state of unity and peace—a place reached not through prideful ambition but through faith, humility, and a willingness to trust in God's plan. The movement from Babel to Zarahemla is not just a physical journey but a spiritual transformation, one that causes us to abandon self-reliance in favor of divine connection.

As we take this journey, Babel invites us to reflect on our own lives: Where does pride lead us to self-reliance rather than seeking divine wisdom? Where does ambition lead us to confusion rather than purpose? By understanding Babel as the starting point, we see that the true purpose of our journey is not to build towers but to build faith, to move from dissonance toward harmony, from fragmentation toward wholeness. Babel may have scattered the people, but it also set them on a path that, with humility and divine guidance, leads toward the clarity, unity, and fulfillment promised in Zarahemla.

Zarahemla as the Spiritual Destination

Zarahemla, nestled in the heart of the Book of Mormon's narrative, represents the "promised land" in its purest form—a destination of divine fulfillment, spiritual refuge, and transformative faith. As the culmination of the Jaredites' journey, Zarahemla is far more than a physical place; it is a profound symbol of what it means to live in harmony with God's guidance. For the Jaredites, Zarahemla offered a new beginning and an opportunity to build a community on principles of resilience, faith, and humility. For modern readers, Zarahemla shines as a beacon, a reminder that, though our personal journeys may be filled with challenges, there exists a destination of inner peace, strength, and divine connection waiting for those who seek it sincerely.

In its essence, Zarahemla is a place prepared for the humble, for those willing to endure, to seek, and to be shaped by divine guidance. It is a land that rewards not just arrival but the qualities cultivated along the way: humility, resilience, and an openness to

God's will. For the people who settled there, Zarahemla became a sanctuary of faith, a place where their commitment to God could flourish. It was a land that brought together diverse groups—the Nephites, Mulekites, and eventually the record of the Jaredites—each contributing to a community united by shared dedication to higher principles. In this way, Zarahemla became a symbol of faith-led resilience, an enduring reminder that those who seek God's path will find a place prepared for them.

But Zarahemla's significance extends beyond a historical gathering place. Spiritually, Zarahemla represents an inner state of peace and fulfillment—a destination of the soul. Just as the Jaredites traveled through hardship and uncertainty to arrive in Zarahemla, so too do we embark on journeys filled with challenges and unknowns, seeking a place of spiritual unity and divine connection. Zarahemla invites us to see that every step, every moment of endurance and faith, draws us closer to our own "promised land," a place of profound connection with God and with ourselves.

For each reader, Zarahemla symbolizes the personal destination we yearn for - a state of spiritual rest where faithfulness meets fulfillment and trust in divine guidance brings lasting peace. It is a place within, a place we arrive at when we lay down pride, embracing humility, and letting our lives be directed by something greater than ourselves. Whether that journey takes the form of overcoming personal struggles, deepening our faith, or building communities rooted in unity and compassion, Zarahemla stands as a reminder that God has prepared a place for each of us.

This journey leads us to move from the confusion of human ambition to the clarity of divine purpose, from the scattering of voices to the unity found in faith. Zarahemla, then, is not just the end of a journey; it is the culmination of our deepest spiritual aspirations, a place where we find peace, purpose, and connection with the divine. This promised land invites each of us to come as we are, to be refined along the way, and to arrive ready to embrace the gifts of faith, resilience, and unity that await in our own spiritual Zarahemla.

The Jaredite Journey as a Universal Spiritual Path

The story of the Jaredites in the Book of Ether is a tale of epic proportions, chronicling a journey of faith, resilience, and transformation that begins in the ambitious towers of Babel and leads to a land of promise across unknown waters. Yet, as vast as their journey is in scope, the Jaredite experience speaks to something deeply personal and universally relevant—the quest for divine guidance, the trials that test our faith, and the path of humility and repentance that leads us back to peace. The Jaredite journey is not just ancient history; it is a map for the soul, a guide to navigate the spiritual journeys that each of us faces in our own way.

Central to the Jaredite story are timeless themes that resonate across faiths and cultures: faith, divine guidance, preparation, humility, and repentance. Their journey begins with a prayer for preservation amidst the confusion of Babel, where the brother of Jared prays for divine intervention to keep his family united. What follows is a path laden with moments that test their faith, calling on them to prepare for an unknown future with courage and resourcefulness. The Jaredites' journey embodies the essential truth that divine guidance is available to those who seek it sincerely but that trust in God requires humility, patience, and, often, great endurance.

As readers engage with the Jaredite journey, they will find insights drawn from world religions—Judaism, Christianity, Islam, Hinduism, and Buddhism—that reveal just how universal these principles are. Across these faiths, we encounter shared beliefs in the power of prayer to connect us with the divine, the importance of humility in seeking wisdom, and the transformative nature of repentance. By drawing these perspectives together, this exploration shows that the Jaredite path is not limited to any single tradition; it reflects the universal spiritual path, one that invites each of us to find our "promised land" through lives marked by faith, resilience, and spiritual growth.

Throughout this book, readers will be guided through the Jaredite story not only as a historical narrative but as a practical spiritual guide, one that offers actionable insights and reflections at each stage. Just as the Jaredites prepared barges to cross a "great deep," we, too, are called to prepare our own vessels of faith, courage, and humility to navigate life's challenges. The Jaredite journey demonstrates that even in our most uncertain moments, divine guidance is present and that, by following it, we can move from confusion toward purpose, from pride toward humility, and from separation toward unity with God and our true selves.

As you read, you will be invited to see your own life in the story of the Jaredites to embrace their journey as a mirror of your spiritual path. From Babel's dissonance to Zarahemla's peace, this journey is a testament to the enduring power of faith and the beauty of trusting a divine plan. The Jaredite journey calls each of us forward, reminding us that the challenges we face are steppingstones on the path to divine fulfillment and that every step brings us closer to our own promised land.

Part I

Divine Guidance and Spiritual Foundations

Introduction

Every journey worth taking begins with a solid foundation, and for the Jaredites, the first bricks were laid in faith and divine guidance. In Part I, *Divine Guidance and Spiritual Foundations*, we explore the roots of their remarkable story, one that begins in the midst of Babel's confusion and evolves into an extraordinary testament to spiritual resilience and preparation. It is here, in these initial steps, that the Jaredites learn a lesson as old as creation - true progress begins by seeking divine direction and cultivating the spiritual tools that will see them through life's "great deeps." This part invites readers to reflect on their own beginnings, grounding their journey in the principles of faith, prayer, and trust in God's wisdom.

At Babel, the Jaredites face a world thrown into chaos, and it is in this moment of collective disarray that they turn to the one source of unwavering guidance: God. In an act of profound faith, the brother of Jared prays for protection and unity, setting the course for the Jaredites' journey and teaching us that no matter where we begin, reaching our destination requires a divine roadmap. The brother of Jared's prayer for his people is a reminder that faith opens doors even in the darkest of times and that God's guidance is there for those who sincerely seek it. With each prayer, the Jaredites demonstrate the essential truth that faith is not passive—it is active, resilient, and brave.

As the story unfolds, we see that divine guidance often asks us to act. God does not merely show the brother of Jared the way; He invites him to build, to create, and to prepare vessels for crossing an unknown sea. These barges, crafted through a mixture of faith, ingenuity, and hard work, become more than physical vessels; they are symbols of the spiritual preparation that the Jaredites will need to endure their journey. In this, the story offers a universal insight: God gives us tools, but it is up to us to prepare ourselves, to build vessels strong enough to withstand the storms of life. Just as the Jaredites prepared their barges, we too, must prepare our faith, cultivating resilience, humility, and trust in divine wisdom.

Part I is a call for us to look inward, to build the foundational practices that anchor our lives and strengthen our connection to God. Through the lenses of Judaism, Christianity, Islam, Hinduism, and Buddhism, we see that prayer, preparation, and trust in divine guidance are principles shared across cultures and time. These are the universal cornerstones of a life well-lived, of a journey that leads to peace, purpose, and the fulfillment of a higher calling.

As you dive into Part I, consider the foundations you are laying in your own life. What "barges" are you building to carry you through life's great seas? How are you inviting divine guidance into your daily path? This section is more than an introduction to the Jaredite story; it is an invitation to embark on your own journey with a renewed focus on the divine guidance and spiritual foundations that make all the difference. In these early steps of faith and preparation, we discover that our journeys, like those of the Jaredites, are led by a guiding hand that is as wise as it is constant, steering us toward a destination beyond our imagining.

Foundations of Faith—Prayer and Divine Preservation

The journey from Babel to Zarahemla begins not with grand plans or miraculous signs but with something deceptively simple: a heartfelt prayer. In the Book of Ether, we meet the brother of Jared as he stands amid the confusion and disarray of Babel's divided tongues. Amidst this chaos, he does not panic; he prays. With humility and boldness, he asks God to preserve the language of his family and their unity, seeking divine protection from the fragmentation unfolding around him. This prayer for preservation becomes a cornerstone for the Jaredites' journey—a moment that highlights the power of sincere requests to connect us with the divine, even in our most uncertain times.

In this chapter, we examine the brother of Jared's prayer as more than a simple request for help; it is an act of deep faith that reminds us of the profound connection between prayer and divine preservation. In a world where languages are scattered, his plea for unity serves as a powerful testament to what can happen when we approach God with pure intent. It is not just a prayer for protection it is a prayer that strengthens the foundation of an entire people's spiritual journey. And it is a lesson for all of us: no matter the noise or confusion around us, we can find clarity, connection, and guidance by sincerely reaching out to God.

The power of prayer as a means of preservation is a theme that resonates deeply across major faith traditions. In Judaism, prayer (*tefillah*) has long been a way of seeking God's protection and connection, a practice as ancient as the Psalms, where David's petitions for divine help echoed through generations. In times of uncertainty, Jewish prayers often seek to preserve both individual faith and communal unity, emphasizing that God is a protector, a "refuge and strength, a very present help in trouble" (Psalm 46:1). Similarly, the Amidah prayer, central to Jewish liturgy, is a structured plea for divine preservation and blessing, embodying the faith that God listens and responds to sincere prayers.

In Christianity, Jesus teaches that prayer is an open door to divine preservation and peace. In the Lord's Prayer, He instructs His followers to pray for protection and deliverance from "evil," showing that asking for divine help is an essential part of our relationship with God. This idea is seen powerfully in the New Testament, where prayer is portrayed as a source of strength, a means to remain grounded in faith, and a way to find peace amid trials. For Christians, prayer is not just a ritual; it is a living connection with God and a source of preservation through the uncertainties of life.

Islam, too, holds prayer (*salat* and *du'a*) as a sacred means of connecting with Allah, who is compassionate, ever-listening, and responsive. In Surah Al-Baqarah (2:186), Allah reassures believers, saying, "When My servants ask you concerning Me, I am indeed close: I listen to the prayer of every suppliant when they call on Me." Here, the assurance of divine preservation is tied directly to the act of prayer, showing that reaching out to Allah can bring unity, peace, and resilience even in challenging times. Muslims believe that through sincere du'a, one can seek not only personal preservation but also protection and unity for family, community, and even humanity.

Together, these faith traditions remind us that prayer is more than a spiritual exercise; it is a profound source of preservation, a way to invoke divine clarity and peace. Just as the brother of Jared's prayer for language preservation kept his family united in purpose, so too can our prayers keep us grounded, resilient, and connected to something greater. When faced with our own moments of disarray or division, we can remember that God hears our prayers—whether whispered in the quiet of the night, chanted in ancient rites, or spoken aloud in times of need. The brother of Jared's example encourages us to approach prayer as an active expression of faith and trust, a way to seek divine guidance and find stability in an unpredictable world.

In our lives as well, prayer can be a stabilizing force, a way to bridge the gap between confusion and clarity, between uncertainty and trust. Consider this: What are the areas in your life where you seek preservation? Where do you feel the need for divine protection, unity, or peace? As you reflect on these questions, remember that prayer offers a direct path to God's presence and support, helping us to rise above the noise and find strength.

As we further into the Jaredite journey, remember that every great journey begins with a foundation of faith, built brick by brick in moments of prayer. The brother of Jared teaches us that even amidst Babel's chaos, a simple, heartfelt prayer can alter the course of history—not only preserving a family's unity but opening a pathway to a promised land. As we seek our own promised lands, may we do so with the same humility, boldness, and faith that characterized the brother of Jared's prayer, trusting that divine preservation is only a prayer away.

Building Barges and Building Faith—Preparation for Life's Journey

When the Lord instructs the brother of Jared to build barges to cross the "great deep," He gives more than just a construction assignment. In this pivotal moment from Ether 2:16–25, God invites the brother of Jared into a powerful partnership, one that requires agency, ingenuity, and trust. These barges, designed to carry the Jaredites across uncharted waters, are more than vessels; they are symbols of faith and preparation. They remind us that while God may provide guidance, He also calls us to actively prepare for our journeys ahead, blending divine insight with our unique skills and efforts.

The brother of Jared's response to this command offers a blueprint for building faith in real, actionable ways. God does not deliver a step-by-step manual. Instead, He challenges the brother of Jared to think creatively, to solve problems, and to seek inspiration. In the process, the brother of Jared learns that true faith is not passive—it is dynamic, adaptive, and deeply involved. The Lord's instructions to "prepare" the vessels show that our faith journey requires our own contributions. Preparation is as much about the heart and mind as it is about physical readiness, and God values our willingness to engage, experiment, and grow.

The brother of Jared's experience mirrors the timeless teachings found in Hinduism and Buddhism, which emphasize the balance between divine guidance and human effort. In Hindu philosophy, the concept of *dharma*, or duty, illustrates this balance. *Dharma* represents each person's sacred responsibility—a calling to act with purpose, honor, and integrity. The Bhagavad Gita, a key Hindu scripture, illustrates this beautifully through the warrior Arjuna's journey, where he learns that his duty is to act with faith and devotion, trusting in divine wisdom but fulfilling his own role. Just as the brother of Jared builds his barges with diligence, Arjuna steps forward in faith, embracing his duty with courage. The message is clear: divine support flows most fully when we act with a purpose, prepare with integrity, and fulfill our unique roles.

Buddhist teachings also offer profound insights into the brother of Jared's journey, particularly through the concept of *right effort*, which is part of the Noble Eightfold Path. In Buddhism, *right effort* means channeling our energies wisely, being proactive in the pursuit of wisdom and compassion, and balancing personal discipline with openness to spiritual insights. Buddha taught that spiritual progress requires effort, intention, and resilience—qualities the brother of Jared embodies as he designs the barges, innovating solutions to ensure his people's safety. This active engagement with his journey reflects the Buddhist principle that while the path may be marked by divine support, it is walked by our own steps.

As we reflect on the brother of Jared's experience, we are invited to consider our own "barges" and the preparation required for the "great deeps" we face. Preparation is about more than physical readiness; it is about building spiritual resilience, honing personal strengths, and embracing the gifts and resources we have been given. Where in your life do you recognize a calling to prepare? What "barges" do you need to build to cross the uncertain waters ahead? Preparation does not mean having all the answers; it means taking deliberate steps, one at a time, using both faith and practical action as guiding forces.

Think about how creativity plays a role in your preparations. The brother of Jared did not just build according to exact specifications; he used his ingenuity to find solutions for light and air, seeking God's insight along the way. In the same way, we are called to actively participate in our journeys, trusting that God will guide us but also valuing the wisdom and creativity we bring to the process. Like the brother of Jared, we may find that as we move forward, our faith deepens, our skills grow, and our vision expands.

The "great deeps" may take many forms in our lives—career changes, family challenges, personal loss, or the pursuit of a meaningful calling. Each of these requires preparation that combines practical action with spiritual readiness. Building faith is like building a barge: it takes time, it involves problem-solving, and it asks us to trust in God's design even when we do not fully understand the journey ahead. The story of the brother of Jared teaches us that faith is a collaborative journey where God's guidance meets our effort, our vision, and our hands.

As you ponder this chapter, take time to identify the areas where you feel called to prepare. How are you combining your faith with action? Are you using the talents and insights God has given you to face life's uncertainties? In building your own "barges," remember that every nail driven, every plank laid, is part of a larger journey toward faith and resilience. Preparation is not just a task; it is a sacred act that strengthens our souls, fortifies our faith, and draws us closer to the divine.

Through the brother of Jared's story, we see that preparation is both a duty and a blessing—a way to align our purpose with God's plan and to step forward with courage into the unknown. As you build your own foundations, you may find strength in knowing that just like the brother of Jared, you are never alone. With faith as your guide and effort as your vessel, you are prepared to cross any "great deep" that lies ahead.

Summary

As we reach the end of Part I, *Divine Guidance and Spiritual Foundations*, we stand alongside the brother of Jared and his people, gazing out across the horizon of their uncharted journey. With prayer as their anchor and carefully crafted barges as their vessels, they are prepared to face the unknown with a faith built on divine guidance and active preparation. In these foundational moments, the Jaredites' journey reminds us that faith is not simply a quiet belief or passive trust; it is a dynamic partnership with God, one that calls for both surrender and action, both seeking and doing.

In exploring these early chapters of the Jaredite story, we have seen how divine guidance constitutes receiving direction while still taking responsibility. The brother of Jared's prayer for preservation amidst Babel's chaos is a testament to the power of sincere, humble requests to invite God's protection and unity. His later preparations for the "great deep," building barges through inspiration and ingenuity demonstrate how God values our creative engagement with His plans. Faith, as these stories reveal, is not the absence of uncertainty but the presence of trust strong enough to propel us forward, even when we cannot see the entire path.

The wisdom drawn from world religions throughout this section enriches our understanding of these foundational principles. In Judaism, Christianity, and Islam, we find that prayer is a bridge to the divine—a sacred moment where we align our intentions with God's will and seek preservation through His strength. From Hinduism and Buddhism, we learn that preparation and personal responsibility are essential parts of any spiritual journey. Like the brother of Jared, each of us has a unique *dharma*, a sacred duty to prepare for life's challenges with integrity, creativity, and resilience.

These principles—prayer, preparation, and divine partnership form the bedrock of our spiritual journeys, and they continue to shape us as we set out toward our own "promised lands." The Jaredites' willingness to build and prepare, even in the face of unknown seas, teaches us that divine guidance does not eliminate challenges; it gives us the strength and wisdom to navigate them. With each step forward, their faith grows, as does their ability to trust God more deeply. This growth is both their foundation and their compass, reminding us that true guidance comes when we place ourselves in God's hands, willing to act and to be led.

As we leave Part I, reflect on the foundations you are laying in your own life. Are you building your own "barges" of faith with care and intention? Are you seeking divine guidance not only to comfort you in uncertainty but to empower you to act? The principles of faith, prayer, and preparation are timeless anchors designed to keep us steady in our own "great deeps."

In the journey ahead, may you carry these foundational lessons with you, knowing that every sincere prayer and every careful step of preparation is part of a greater purpose. Like the Jaredites, we may not know every detail of the path before us, but we can trust in a God who guides, strengthens, and preserves those who seek Him. As you move forward, may your faith be your vessel, your preparation be your strength, and your trust in divine guidance be the steady hand that leads you toward your own promised land.

Author's Reflection

As I reflect on Part I, Divine Guidance and Spiritual Foundations, I find myself immersed in the powerful imagery of the journey from Babel to Zarahemla—a journey not just of ancient people but of the individual soul. Standing at Babel amidst the noise and confusion, I feel the weight of life's uncertainties, its moments of division and doubt. It is easy to see Babel as something far removed, a distant story of ancient people. Yet, when I look closer, I see Babel within myself. I recognize that same impulse to reach for lofty heights without a clear purpose, to build out of ambition rather than intention, and to experience times when confusion leaves me grasping for clarity. Babel is the starting point for each of us, and its lessons are as personal as they are universal.

But from Babel, we are given the chance to journey toward something better. For the Jaredites, it was the humbling moment of prayer—an act of surrender that acknowledges our limitations and opens the door to divine help. The brother of Jared's prayer resonates with me deeply because it is a reminder that, even in chaos, there is a voice that always listens, a presence that always guides. His prayer is not just about language or family unity; it is about a choice to move forward with purpose, anchored in faith. As I think about my own life, I ask myself: Where am I choosing purpose over confusion? Where am I turning to divine guidance as I seek unity within myself and clarity in my path? These are the questions that Babel prompts in all of us.

Then comes the task of preparation—a call that echoes through my thoughts with urgency and meaning. The Lord does not simply smooth out the Jaredites' path; He invites them to build, to act, to prepare for the unknown with intention and faith. The brother of Jared's response to this call is nothing short of inspiring. He does not hesitate to pick up tools, to imagine solutions, and to construct something entirely new. His faith is not merely a belief—it is active, resilient, and practical. In my own journey, I see this as a call to action: to build my own "barges" of faith, those tools and habits that will carry me across life's "great deeps." Whether it is through prayer, self-reflection, or seeking out wisdom from others, I am reminded that I, too, have the responsibility to prepare to use the resources and abilities God has given me.

I think about the different roles that faith and preparation play in my life. Faith can be the comforting thought, the steady voice of assurance, the presence of peace. But preparation? Preparation is the daily work, the act of building, the courageous decision to put faith into motion. The brother of Jared's journey shows me that real faith is more than a feeling—it is a practice, a discipline, a commitment to create something sturdy enough to weather the storms. It is humbling to recognize that God does not ask for perfection; He asks for effort, for willingness to engage in the process, even when the outcome is unknown.

As I reflect on these stories, I am not just reading about the Jaredites. I am stepping into their footsteps, finding my own journey from Babel to Zarahemla, and understanding that the pathway to the promised land is built on these simple yet profound acts: praying with humility, preparing with intention, and trusting in divine guidance every step of the way. The foundation stones of faith and preparation are set with each prayer, each moment of action, and each instance where I choose to move forward with God as my guide.

In a world filled with its own modern "Babels"—the distractions, the divisions, the noise of ambition—I realize that the journey to Zarahemla is more relevant than ever. It is the journey to a place of peace, unity, and divine connection, a place I carry within myself when I am willing to follow God's guidance and do the work He asks of me. In this way, Zarahemla is not just a distant land or a promised destination; it is a spiritual reality, one that I can live each day through my choices, my faith, and my efforts to build a life rooted in divine guidance.

The journey from Babel to Zarahemla is the journey of the soul, one that, even with its challenges, brings me closer to purpose, to peace, and to the God who walks beside me.

Part II

Revelation and Unveiling Divine Truths

Introduction

If the first steps of the Jaredite journey taught us to listen for divine guidance and prepare with faith, Part II, *Revelation and Unveiling Divine Truths*, draws us deeper into the mystery of faith. This part of the journey is not simply about moving forward; it is about seeing with new eyes and learning to recognize the divine even when it is obscured by the "veil of unbelief." Here, the Jaredite narrative invites us to explore the transformative power of revelation—the moments when faith is not only acted upon but answered in ways that illuminate our path and alter the course of our lives.

The brother of Jared's experience of revelation marks a turning point in the Jaredite journey, one that begins with a humble request for light and ends in an encounter with the Divine itself. It is a powerful reminder that, as we pursue our journeys of faith, God often meets us in ways we cannot anticipate. Revelation is not always a grand proclamation; sometimes, it is as simple—and as miraculous—as a touch of light in the dark. Yet, as we learn from the brother of Jared, such light requires both the courage to ask and the faith to believe it will be given.

This part of the Jaredite story asks us to examine the nature of revelation and what it means to see God more clearly in our own lives. Through his profound faith, the brother of Jared becomes a witness to divine truths, unveiling what is usually hidden. His story compels us to ask: What veils are we willing to uncover to see the truth more clearly? Where are we holding back, and what would it take to approach God with the same humility and courage that he did? In learning to unveil divine truths, we discover that God's presence is not distant or elusive; it is near, responsive, and deeply personal.

Revelation has always been a bridge across the ages, a way for God to communicate eternal truths to His children. In the teachings of world religions, this theme resonates profoundly. In Christianity, Jesus promises that those who seek will find. Revelation comes to those who knock with faith. In Islam, the Quran is viewed as the ultimate revelation, given to illuminate and guide. In Hinduism and Buddhism, revelation often emerges through meditation, self-discovery, and enlightenment, showing that divine truths can be uncovered through both inner reflection and divine inspiration. In this section, the Jaredite story harmonizes with these traditions, illustrating that while the means of revelation may differ, the essence of divine truth remains universal.

As we journey through Part II, we are invited to seek beyond mere guidance; we are encouraged to ask to see. Revelation requires us to actively engage our faith, to trust that when we seek divine truth, God will answer with light. The brother of Jared's experience shows us that divine truths are not solely reserved for prophets of ancient times—they are accessible to anyone willing to seek with sincerity and act with faith. His story is a call to each of us to open our hearts, to approach God boldly yet humbly, and to trust that He is willing to reveal His light when we are ready to receive it.

So, as we move into Part II, consider what revelations you might seek in your own life. What questions are pressing on your heart? What answers are you hoping to find? This section is an invitation to let go of doubts, step forward with trust, and to believe that God's truths—personal, illuminating, and life-changing—are within reach. When we are willing to rend the veil of unbelief, we discover that revelation is not an event from the distant past; it is a living, present reality that can light our way to the promised lands of understanding, peace, and divine connection.

Rending the Veil—Faith as a Gateway to Revelation

In one of the most striking moments of the Book of Mormon, the brother of Jared's faith pierces through the veil of mortality, granting him a vision of the Lord Himself. In Ether 3, what begins as a humble request for light transforms into one of the most profound encounters with the divine in all scripture. With a faith so powerful it dissolves barriers, the brother of Jared witnesses the Lord, beholding not only God's glory but also a glimpse into eternity. This scene is more than just a revelation; it is a lesson in how faith can become a gateway to truth, a key that unlocks what is hidden. Through the brother of Jared's example, we learn that true revelation is not an accidental gift—it is the result of persistent and steadfast faith, a trust so strong it parts even the densest veils of doubt.

The brother of Jared's extraordinary encounter challenges us to consider: What veils cloud our own vision? Where do we hold back in faith, allowing doubt or fear to obscure the clarity we seek? His story shows us that revelation is not a matter of chance; it is an invitation to each of us to approach God with trust, humility, and openness to whatever truths He may reveal. It is about letting go of the uncertainties that weigh us down, releasing our tight grip on doubt, and embracing a faith that clears the way for divine light to break through.

This theme of "rending the veil" is echoed across world religions, where the journey from doubt to understanding is a sacred path. In Christianity, Jesus encourages His followers to ask, seek, and knock, promising that those who seek with sincere hearts will find (Matthew 7:7–8). The Apostle Paul speaks of faith as "the substance of things hoped for, the evidence of things not seen" (Hebrews 11:1). This faith, which Paul describes, is not passive; it is active, it requires intention, and it is a force that opens doors to understanding. In the teachings of The Church of Jesus Christ of Latter-day Saints, this principle is echoed in the invitation to "ask in faith, nothing wavering" (James 1:6). Revelation, according to LDS teachings, is available to anyone who approaches God with a heart open to truth and a willingness to act on what they receive.

In Buddhism, while the language differs, the principles resonate. The concept of enlightenment (*bodhi*)—achieving clarity and spiritual insight—often comes through *vipassana* meditation, a practice that clears the mind and allows one to see reality as it truly is. Buddhist meditation is a process of rending internal veils, the mental fog of attachment, desire, and fear, to achieve a state of openness and presence. Through meditation, practitioners cultivate awareness, gradually moving beyond doubt to experience clarity and wisdom. In this sense, enlightenment in Buddhism parallels the act of rending the veil: it is a process of transcending our limited perspectives to see with the eyes of understanding and truth.

What all these traditions teach us is that revelation—whether seen as divine guidance, enlightenment, or spiritual insight—requires more than wishful thinking. It requires intention, humility, and, most importantly, faith. And faith is not about having all the answers; it is about trusting enough to seek the answers, to step into the unknown with confidence that light will eventually come. The brother of Jared's experience shows us that when we are willing to believe, when we approach God with unshakeable faith, He is more than willing to unveil His presence.

So how can we, like the brother of Jared, rend the veils that may cloud our own path? First, it begins with a choice to approach God with humility. When we come before God with a heart open to whatever He may reveal, we surrender our own assumptions and agendas, creating space for divine light to enter. Second, it requires trust—a willingness to believe that God will respond, even if we cannot yet see how. Faith is an act of courage, of opening ourselves to truths that may stretch us, challenge us, and ultimately transform us.

Finally, rending the veil of doubt means letting go of the need for perfect clarity before we act. The brother of Jared did not wait for an assurance of what he would see; he approached the Lord with faith and was rewarded with a revelation more profound than he could have imagined. In our own lives, we often wait for the perfect conditions to seek answers or clarity. However, the story of the brother of Jared reminds us that faith often precedes understanding that sometimes, we must move forward, trusting that revelation will come as we go.

As you reflect on this chapter, consider the areas in your life where doubt holds you back. What would it take for you to approach God with the same humble courage as the brother of Jared? Where can you set aside fear and step forward in faith, trusting that as you seek, God will reveal? This is the essence of rending the veil—to trust that, even if we cannot yet see, we are seen, heard, and guided by a God who is near and eager to reveal His presence.

The journey of revelation is one that requires patience, openness, and a willingness to let go of our need for control. But when we do, the reward is profound. Like the brother of Jared, we, too, can experience divine truths that fill our lives with light, guidance, and purpose. When we are willing to rend the veil of doubt, we discover that revelation is not a distant promise; it is a present reality, one that beckons each of us to draw near, to ask, and to receive.

The Role of Witnesses—Community and the Confirmation of Truth

In Ether 5, Moroni introduces the concept of the Three Witnesses, a principle that reverberates through history, faith, and community. He prophesies that three individuals will see the plates from which the Book of Mormon is translated, adding their voices to his own. This is more than a footnote in history; it is a profound statement about the nature of truth itself. Through the Three Witnesses, Moroni demonstrates that the strongest truths often require multiple voices—a communal confirmation that resonates far beyond any single individual's experience. This chapter invites us to reflect on the role of witnesses in our lives, the significance of shared testimony, and the impact that bearing our personal witness has on strengthening faith both within ourselves and in the hearts of others.

The idea of communal witness is timeless, stretching across cultures and faiths. In Jewish tradition, the law requires two or three witnesses to establish truth, emphasizing that the voices of others add weight and credibility. Deuteronomy 19:15 declares, "A matter must be established by the testimony of two or three witnesses," underscoring the importance of shared witness as a foundation for community trust and ethical grounding. This is not just a rule of law; it reflects how deeply interwoven our lives are and how truth gains strength when shared and affirmed by others.

In Islam, the principle of communal witness takes on a profound significance as well. The *Shahada*, the central declaration of faith, is itself a form of testimony: "There is no god but Allah, and Muhammad is His Messenger." This declaration is not simply personal; it is recited in the presence of others, symbolizing unity and shared commitment to truth. Islam also emphasizes the concept of *shahadah* (bearing witness) in legal and ethical matters, requiring witnesses to validate contracts, agreements, and other significant events. Just as Moroni calls upon witnesses to affirm the Book of Mormon's truth, Islamic teachings remind us that the presence of witnesses strengthens bonds of trust and community, reflecting the belief that truth grows clearer when shared.

Buddhism, too, values the power of communal witness in a different yet complementary way. The concept of *sangha*, or spiritual community, is one of the "Three Jewels" of Buddhism, emphasizing that the path to enlightenment is not a solitary pursuit. Buddhists often gather to recite teachings, reflect, and offer mutual support, bearing witness to each other's progress and growth. The *sangha* serves as a community of witnesses, affirming each person's journey and collectively strengthening the resolve of each individual. Here, communal witness becomes a means of shared accountability, compassion, and encouragement.

What Moroni, and indeed these world religions, teach us is that truth is often more powerful and lasting when it is witnessed by others. Individual experience is valuable, but shared witness elevates that experience into something that can guide, inspire, and reassure a community. When we bear witness to our faith—whether through testimony, lived example, or shared values—we add our voice to a chorus that echoes through time, connecting us with those who have come before us and those who will follow. By participating in this web of shared truth, we create a foundation upon which faith can stand firm, even in times of uncertainty.

Moroni's invitation to communal witness is also a call to each of us. Bearing witness does not have to be grand or dramatic. Sometimes, it is as simple as sharing a personal insight, recounting a moment of guidance, or living in a way that reflects our values.

When we share our testimonies, even in small ways, we contribute to a collective strength that sustains and uplifts those around us. Each of us has a story, an experience, or a piece of wisdom that can serve as a light for someone else.

So, how do we bear personal witness in a meaningful way? First, it begins with authenticity. Sharing our witness does not require polished words or perfect experience; it requires honesty and sincerity. When we speak from the heart, others can feel the truth of our experiences, and our words resonate on a deeper level. Second, bearing witness involves courage. Like Moroni, we may not know the full impact our words will have, but we trust that sharing our testimony will strengthen both ourselves and others. Finally, bearing witness requires humility. It is not about proclaiming ourselves as the sole holders of truth; it is about adding our voices to a greater truth that transcends any single perspective.

In sharing our faith and experiences, we create connections that reach beyond ourselves. We help others feel less alone in their journeys, reminding them that faith is a shared endeavor, a mosaic of individual insights that together create a fuller picture of divine truth. As Moroni's prophecy of the Three Witnesses shows, our testimonies are more than personal declarations—they are gifts to others, affirmations that faith is real, and evidence that God's presence can be felt, even in the quietest moments.

As you consider the role of witnesses in your own life, ask yourself: Where can I share my experiences to strengthen someone else's faith? What moments of guidance or peace can I offer as a witness to the goodness of God? Remember, your testimony is not only valuable for your own spiritual journey; it is a source of light and strength for others who may be seeking their own confirmation of truth.

In this chapter, Moroni reminds us that truth becomes even more powerful when shared and that our testimonies are essential to a community of faith. By embracing the role of witness, each of us becomes part of something larger, a tapestry of voices that testifies to divine truths transcending time, culture, and circumstances. Let your voice join this chorus, bearing witness to the truths that guide your life and, in doing so, illuminate the path for those who walk alongside you.

Summary

As we reach the end of Part II, *Revelation and Unveiling Divine Truths*, we stand in awe at the power of faith to lift the veil between the seen and the unseen, the known and the unknown. The brother of Jared's extraordinary journey in these pages has shown us that revelation is not a passive gift bestowed only upon prophets of old; it is an active pursuit, a process we engage in with courage, openness, and unwavering faith. We learn that the divine is never far off but waits for us to seek and trust deeply enough to see beyond our mortal limits.

The brother of Jared's encounter with the Lord stands as one of the most profound demonstrations of what faith can accomplish when it is free of doubt and rich with expectancy. His remarkable vision reminds us that true revelation often requires us to step forward even when we do not see the whole path. It also encourages us to trust in divine answers even when we cannot predict the questions. And the moment we dare to seek God wholeheartedly, with every ounce of faith we possess, He will meet us with light, clarity, and truth.

But divine revelation is not solely a private experience. As we explored in the concept of the Three Witnesses, the confirmation of truth finds its fullest expression within a community of believers. Moroni's prophecy of the Three Witnesses in Ether 5 reaffirms that truth becomes more powerful and enduring when it is shared, acknowledged, and supported by others. Revelation, then, is not just the opening of divine truths to one individual but an invitation to participate in a greater, collective testimony—a chorus of voices that unites to proclaim God's presence, goodness, and guidance. This call to communal witness reminds us that each of us has a role in building a community rooted in faith and shared truth.

Across faith traditions, the theme of revelation holds a powerful place. In Christianity, revelation is often seen as a personal relationship with God, a journey through which divine truths unfold in the heart and guide the path ahead. In Buddhism, enlightenment is a process of shedding the self to see reality as it truly is, a revelation achieved through deep reflection and meditation. In Islam, the Quran is the ultimate revelation, illuminating the way for believers through sacred guidance. In each of these traditions, we see echoes of the brother of Jared's journey that teach us that unveiling divine truths requires faith, humility, and a readiness to act upon what we are shown.

As we close this part of the journey, let us carry forward the lessons of revelation into our own lives. The brother of Jared's story invites us to seek God with an open heart, to ask questions boldly yet humbly, and to expect that answers will come, sometimes in ways we may not anticipate. Revelation, as we have seen, is less about the mechanics of asking and more about the readiness to receive. It is about letting go of the veils of doubt, fear, and distraction that obscure our vision and allowing God's light to illuminate our path.

Consider how your own revelations might serve as a source of strength for others. Whether through a spoken testimony, a quiet example, or an act of kindness, you have the power to bear witness to the divine truths you have experienced, adding your voice to the eternal witness that surrounds us all. Like Moroni's prophecy of the Three Witnesses, your testimony becomes a link in a chain of faith, one that reinforces and uplifts, which inspires and confirms.

In the journey ahead, may you find the courage to seek God's truths with your whole heart, the humility to receive them with gratitude, and the wisdom to share them with others. Revelation is not a distant promise; it is a present reality, a gift waiting to be unveiled as we approach God with faith. And as we journey toward our own promised lands, let us remember that we are never alone. We walk in the light of those who came before us, surrounded by a community of believers who, together, continue to unveil the divine truths that guide us all.

Author's Reflection

As I look back on Part II, Revelation and Unveiling Divine Truths, I realize that the journey from Babel to Zarahemla is as much a journey of sight as it is of faith. Revelation is woven through this part of the Jaredite story, but it is not something passive that merely happens to them—it is something they actively seek and prepare themselves to receive. Standing with the brother of Jared as he approaches God, I cannot help but feel the significance of his faith. He does not just ask; he asks with a belief so solid, a desire so sincere, that the veil of mortality itself is dissolved, and he sees the Lord. His example invites me to reflect on my own journey, asking myself what veils I am willing—and ready—to part in order to gain clearer insight into the divine.

The brother of Jared's revelation began with a simple request for light. That is how revelation often starts, isn't it? A desire for guidance, a need for answers, or a plea for understanding in the midst of uncertainty. Like him, I also have moments where I'm just asking for a little light—a glimmer of insight, a spark of reassurance in a world that sometimes feels dim and overwhelming. But his story shows me that when faith is woven with action, something far more transformative is possible. There is a difference between wanting light and being ready to see it, and the brother of Jared's readiness is what leads him to behold the Lord Himself. It makes me wonder: How ready am I to understand clearly what I am asking for? Am I willing to let my faith be active, to step forward even without perfect clarity?

Revelation, as I have learned in reflecting on this part of the Jaredite story, is not about obtaining information—it is about opening ourselves up to something greater, a process that requires humility, trust, and courage. I see this mirrored across the world's great spiritual traditions, each one offering its own path to clarity. In Christianity, the call to "ask, seek, and knock" reminds me that revelation is both invitation and response, a process that grows deeper the more we engage in it. Buddhism teaches that through practices like meditation and reflection, we gradually unveil truth, clearing the mind of distractions to see with a clarity that transforms. In both these perspectives, revelation is not only about the light itself but about our willingness to create space within ourselves to receive it.

This understanding has reshaped the way I view my own moments of doubt and questioning. Rather than waiting for answers to descend, I am learning to approach them as opportunities for growth, chances to "rend the veil" of my own uncertainties and open my heart to God's truths. It is humbling to realize that revelation requires as much from us as it offers. It is an invitation to step beyond comfort and to trust that the unknown can lead us to greater understanding. The brother of Jared's courage to approach the Lord reminds me that true revelation is not afraid of what it might find; it seeks boldly, ready to accept whatever God has to show.

Then there is the role of shared witness, a reminder that revelation, while deeply personal, finds its fullest expression within community. The brother of Jared's encounter with the Lord is a sacred moment, but Moroni's prophecy of the Three Witnesses adds a new dimension, underscoring that truth often gains its strength when it is shared. This resonates deeply with me. In a world that values individuality, it is easy to forget that our experiences are woven into a larger tapestry of faith. By bearing witness, we not only affirm our own truths but reinforce them for others. I am reminded that my own moments of revelation are not just mine to keep—they are gifts meant to be shared, links in a chain of faith that stretches far beyond myself.

As I move forward, the lessons from Part II stay with me. Revelation is both a process and a responsibility, a call to open myself to God's truths and to trust in the light He is ready to give. But it is also a call to be a witness, to add my voice to the many who testify of faith and light, building a community where truth is both personal and shared. In my own journey from Babel to Zarahemla, I see that the veils I choose to part reveal not only insights into my path but also the profound interconnectedness of our shared human search for divine understanding. And in that search, I find comfort, knowing that we are all moving toward the same promised land, each of us seeking, each of us unveiling, truths that light the way for one another.

Part III

Leadership Lessons and the Cycles of Faith

Introduction

As we enter Part III, *Leadership Lessons and the Cycles of Faith*, the Jaredite story takes on a new dimension, delving into the challenges and triumphs of leading people across generations. Here, leadership is not just about power or position; it is about purpose and integrity. Through the choices of Jaredite kings—some humble and faithful, others prideful and self-serving—we see that leadership is both a privilege and a responsibility, one that shapes not only the individual leader but also the very fabric of society. In these cycles of faith and pride, righteousness and rebellion, we witness the profound impact that leadership can have on a people's journey toward or away from the promised land.

The stories of leaders like Orihah, Shule, and Coriantumr reveal the profound influence of character on a leader's legacy. When guided by humility, faith, and a commitment to their people's well-being, these leaders establish societies rooted in peace and unity. They understand that leadership is not merely a position to hold but a stewardship to uphold, a call to serve rather than to be served. But alongside these righteous rulers, we also encounter those whose ambition, pride, and disregard for divine principles lead to turmoil and decay. The contrast between these leaders teaches us that faith is not a one-time declaration but an ongoing commitment, one that must be renewed by each generation, each individual, and each leader.

In the cycles of faith and pride that mark Jaredite history, we find lessons echoed across time and culture. From Judaism's teachings on ethical leadership to Christianity's emphasis on servant leadership, to the Buddhist concept of compassionate authority, world religions underscore that leadership grounded in integrity is essential to a society's health and harmony. Islam, too, teaches that leaders are accountable not only to their people but to God, a reminder that true authority comes with divine responsibility. The principles guiding these faith traditions resonate deeply in the Jaredite story, revealing that the values of humility, service, and accountability are timeless, forming the bedrock of any enduring civilization.

Part III invites us to examine not only the qualities that define effective leaders but also the cycles of faith and pride that we, too, navigate in our personal lives. Leadership, after all, is not limited to kings or rulers. Each of us is called to lead in our own spheres— within our families, communities, workplaces, and spiritual lives. The choices we make, the values we uphold, and the priorities we set have a ripple effect on those around us. This section is both a study of ancient leaders and a mirror, asking us to consider: How do we lead? Do we use our influence to uplift and inspire, or do we seek recognition and power at the expense of integrity? The Jaredites' story is a reminder that each choice we make strengthens or weakens the foundations of faith for ourselves and those who follow.

As we move through the cycles of leadership and faith in the Jaredite narrative, we are reminded that each generation faces the same timeless question: Will we choose humility over pride, service over self-interest, and faith over ambition? And perhaps most importantly, are we willing to learn from those who came before us? Part III is an invitation to reflect on our own roles as leaders, to recognize the cycles we encounter, and to find strength in choosing principles that lead not only to success but to lasting peace.

Let this section inspire you to lead with purpose, to serve with compassion, and to navigate the cycles of faith with resilience. The Jaredite kings may have lived long ago, but their lessons on leadership, humility, and the impact of one's choices are as relevant as ever. Together, let us take these lessons to heart, allowing them to shape our journey as we continue toward our own promised lands, guided by the principles that sustain communities and enrich lives for generations to come.

Humility and Righteous Leadership—The Example of Faithful Kings

In the Jaredite narrative, we see that true leadership is not about ruling over others; it is about lifting others up. Leaders like Orihah in Ether 6–7 show us what it means to govern with humility and integrity, fostering peace and prosperity for their people. Orihah, the first king of the Jaredites, emerges as a model of righteous leadership, steering his people with compassion and an unwavering commitment to their well-being. In a time when the trappings of power could easily have led him down a path of pride, Orihah instead chose humility, grounding his leadership in service rather than self-interest. His example speaks across ages and cultures, reminding us that humility is not a weakness in leadership—it is its greatest strength.

The story of Orihah and other faithful Jaredite kings highlights a powerful truth: when leaders prioritize the well-being of those they serve, communities flourish. In contrast to later rulers who would lead with ambition and pride, Orihah's reign was marked by peace and prosperity, not because he sought to make a name for himself but because he led with a sincere desire to honor his people and his God. His humility was not passive; it was an active, conscious choice to govern in a way that uplifted others. This is the kind of leadership that not only builds societies but sustains them, creating a foundation of trust, integrity, and unity.

The qualities Orihah exemplifies are echoed across world religions, where the call to servant leadership is emphasized as essential to ethical and spiritual life. In Christianity, Jesus teaches, "Whoever wants to become great among you must be your servant" (Matthew 20:26). This principle, known as servant leadership, is the heart of Jesus's teachings, where greatness is defined not by authority but by the willingness to serve others. Jesus Himself washed the feet of His disciples, illustrating that true leaders are those who kneel, who reach out in love, and who consider the needs of others above their own. This model of leadership is a profound call to humility, a reminder that authority is not a license to dominate but a responsibility to care.

In Judaism, the concept of humility (*anavah*) is deeply connected to leadership, emphasizing that the greatest leaders are those who view themselves as servants of God and humanity. Figures like Moses are celebrated not only for their accomplishments but for their humility. The Torah describes Moses as "very humble, more than all people" (Numbers 12:3), a leader who, despite his position, maintained a deep sense of responsibility to his people and obedience to God. For Moses, leadership was an act of service, one that required putting aside personal ambition to fulfill a higher purpose. This humility allowed him to guide the Israelites with compassion and resilience, qualities that have set the standard for righteous leadership throughout Jewish history.

In Islam, the idea of *Khilafah* (stewardship) emphasizes that leaders are not owners of power but caretakers entrusted by Allah to act justly and responsibly. The Prophet Muhammad exemplified this principle, often reminding his followers that leaders should serve rather than be served. One of his sayings, "The leader of a people is their servant," underscores that humility and justice are inseparable from true leadership. In the Islamic view, leaders are accountable to God for how they treat others, a powerful reminder that with authority comes the sacred duty to act with kindness, integrity, and a commitment to the greater good.

Reflecting on Orihah's legacy and the insights from these traditions, we see that humility in leadership is not merely about thinking less of oneself—it's about thinking of others more. Leadership grounded in humility does not seek to elevate the self but seeks to elevate those it serves. This principle is as relevant in our own lives as it was in Orihah's kingdom, whether we are leading in our families, our communities, our workplaces, or our spiritual circles. Humility invites us to consider: How can I lead in a way that supports, uplifts, and empowers others? Am I using my influence to serve or to be served?

In our world today, the need for humility and integrity in leadership is more pressing than ever. Whether we hold a formal position or simply influence those around us, we each have the opportunity to practice leadership through service. Just as Orihah's humble reign brought blessings to his people, our own acts of servant leadership can foster trust, resilience, and a sense of community. Leading with humility means listening as much as speaking, valuing others' contributions, and recognizing that leadership is ultimately about guiding others toward their potential.

As you reflect on the example of Orihah and other faithful leaders, consider where you might bring more humility and service into your own life. How can you lead in a way that prioritizes the needs and growth of those around you? Remember, true leadership is not about the recognition we receive but about the impact we leave behind. Just as Orihah's humble leadership became a foundation of peace and prosperity, so too can our own commitment to serve and create a legacy of trust, unity, and compassion in the lives we touch.

In choosing to lead with humility, we follow a path well-trodden by those who understand that greatness is not found in power but in service. Like Orihah, we can cultivate a leadership that seeks the good of others, transforming our families, communities, and organizations into places where faith, integrity, and unity thrive. Let us take this lesson to heart, remembering that the greatest leaders are those who, like Orihah, serve with humility, honoring the sacred responsibility that comes with influence and striving to bless those they lead.

The Cycle of Pride and Corruption—Lessons from the Fall of Leaders

In Ether 7–9, the Jaredite story takes a darker turn, shifting from the humble and faithful reign of Orihah to a tragic descent into pride, corruption, and, ultimately, moral collapse. Leaders like Riplakish exemplify how easily power can corrupt, turning rulers into oppressors and ambition into ruin. Riplakish's reign, marked by vanity and self-serving desires, reveals a truth that echoes through history and across cultures: when pride takes hold, it distorts vision, corrodes integrity, and disrupts communities. In his story, we see the cycle of pride and corruption unfold, a cautionary tale that resonates as strongly today as it did in Jaredite times. Through his example, we are reminded that pride and selfish ambition are the seeds of a leader's downfall, both in ancient kingdoms and in our own lives.

Riplakish's rise and subsequent fall underscore how pride transforms authority into tyranny. What begins as a position of influence becomes a platform for self-gratification, eroding the moral foundations of leadership and exploiting the very people he was meant to protect. His greed and oppressive rule reveal the high costs of self-centered leadership—costs borne not only by the leader but by those they govern. The contrast between Riplakish and the humble kings who preceded him highlights a sobering truth: pride does not simply harm the individual; it unravels the fabric of society, replacing unity with discord and peace with suffering. In Riplakish's story, we see a powerful warning: unchecked ambition and self-serving motives will not lead us to greatness but to isolation, chaos, and eventual collapse.

The destructive consequences of pride are a theme explored across spiritual traditions. Buddhism, for example, teaches that *tanha* (selfish craving or desire) is a primary source of suffering.

Buddha warned that attachment to one's ego and the pursuit of personal gain creates an unending cycle of dissatisfaction and suffering, which extends beyond the individual to harm entire communities. Buddhist teachings advocate for *anatta*, or the principle of "non-self," which encourages individuals to let go of their ego and cultivate compassion, humility, and a focus on the greater good. Just as Riplakish's attachment to power led to his ruin, Buddhism reminds us that a self-centered approach to life ultimately distances us from peace and integrity.

In Hinduism, the principle of *dharma* serves as a guide to avoid the pitfalls of pride and selfish ambition. Dharma refers to the righteous path, a duty to act with moral responsibility and a sense of service toward others. Leaders who align with their dharma are expected to uphold values that benefit the whole rather than serve their own interests. The Hindu epic *Mahabharata* illustrates this through characters who either adhere to or abandon their dharma, showing how pride and the pursuit of personal power disrupt harmony and lead to destruction. In the same way, Riplakish's neglect of any higher duty serves as a reminder that when leaders stray from their moral obligations, they not only harm themselves but disrupt the balance and well-being of their communities.

Latter-day Saint teachings also emphasize the perils of pride, highlighting it as one of the most destructive forces to spiritual growth and community unity. President Ezra Taft Benson, a former

LDS Church leader, called pride "the universal sin," a vice that puts self-interest above divine will and distances individuals from God and each other. In LDS thought, pride is seen as the root of rebellion, the trait that turns hearts away from God and disrupts relationships. The Book of Mormon itself repeatedly warns of the "pride cycle," a recurring pattern where societies fall into prosperity, become prideful, and ultimately descend into conflict and suffering. The story of Riplakish exemplifies this cycle, showing how pride, left unchecked, consumes leaders and societies alike.

These teachings across traditions reveal a shared understanding: pride is not merely a personal flaw but a social toxin. It creates a ripple effect that harms relationships, disrupts communities, and leads to personal and collective suffering. Riplakish's story, along with these teachings, invites each of us to consider the presence of pride in our own lives. Are there areas where ambition overshadows integrity? Or where self-interest takes precedence over the welfare of others? The Jaredite story calls us to look inward, to recognize where pride might be influencing our choices, and to replace it with humility, service, and a commitment to something greater than ourselves.

Taking action against pride begins with awareness—an honest look at where we may be prioritizing our own needs or desires over those around us. Humility, as these traditions teach, is not about self-denial but about shifting focus from self-centered goals to collective well-being. In Buddhism, humility is cultivated through mindfulness, a practice that quiets the ego and fosters compassion. In Hinduism, the concept of *seva* (selfless service) encourages individuals to serve others without expectation, teaching that by uplifting others, we ourselves are uplifted. In Christianity, humility is modeled by Jesus Christ, who taught that "the greatest among you shall be your servant" (Matthew 23:11), showing that true strength lies in lifting others rather than seeking one's own gain.

As you reflect on this chapter, consider where humility might play a greater role in your life. How can you lead with integrity, prioritizing service over self-interest? In what ways can you recognize and combat pride to prevent it from disrupting your relationships, your work, and your personal growth? The story of Riplakish serves as a powerful reminder that true greatness is not achieved through ambition alone but through character, compassion, and a dedication to something beyond oneself.

Ultimately, the cycle of pride and corruption is one we can choose to break. By fostering humility, embracing our responsibility to others, and focusing on the greater good, we not only avoid the pitfalls of leaders like Riplakish, but we create lives marked by integrity and lasting impact. Let the lessons of this chapter encourage you to lead with purpose, to serve with humility, and to live in a way that builds rather than diminishes the world around you. In rejecting pride and choosing humility, we break free from destructive cycles and step into leadership that enriches not only our lives but the lives of all those we touch.

Secret Combinations and Societal Decay-The Dangers of Hidden Corruption

In Ether 8, we encounter one of the darkest elements of the Jaredite narrative: the rise of "secret combinations." These clandestine alliances, marked by secrecy, manipulation, and deceit, serve as a powerful warning about the corrosive nature of hidden corruption. Secret combinations are not just agreements; they are pacts rooted in ambition, greed, and a willingness to achieve power by any means, regardless of the harm inflicted upon society. As these hidden forces take root within the Jaredite civilization, they lead to betrayal, injustice, and, ultimately, the unraveling of an entire nation. The impact is profound, revealing how hidden corruption spreads like a disease, infecting even the most foundational elements of society and eroding trust, unity, and peace.

The destructive potential of secret combinations highlights a timeless truth: corruption, when allowed to grow unchecked, is a force that dismantles from within. The Jaredites' downfall serves as a stark reminder that hidden corruption does not merely affect the individuals who participate in it; it destabilizes communities and undermines the moral fabric of society. In the case of the Jaredites, this hidden corruption becomes a catalyst for societal decay, creating a culture of distrust and perpetuating cycles of violence and betrayal. When leaders prioritize secrecy and self-interest over transparency and collective good, the consequences ripple outward, breeding fear, division, and, ultimately, collapse.

Across religious traditions, the emphasis on honesty, transparency, and accountability stands as a counterpoint to the dangers of hidden corruption. In Islam, honesty (*sidq*) is viewed as a fundamental virtue, and truthfulness is seen as central to a just and healthy society. The Quran warns against deceit, teaching that those who deceive and manipulate act in opposition to God's will. Surah An-Nisa (4:135) calls believers to uphold justice, even when it is difficult, stating, "Stand out firmly for justice, as witnesses to Allah, even if it be against yourselves or your parents or your kin." In Islam, secrecy and corruption are seen as forces that disrupt community harmony, whereas transparency is a form of devotion, aligning oneself with divine truth and fostering trust.

In Judaism, the concept of *emet* (truth) is foundational, underscoring the importance of living with integrity and transparency. The Hebrew Scriptures place a strong emphasis on honesty, justice, and accountability. The prophet Micah admonishes, "What does the Lord require of you but to do justice, and to love kindness, and to walk humbly with your God?" (Micah 6:8). The Torah warns against false witness and hidden schemes, teaching that true leadership is rooted in honesty and righteousness. In Jewish thought, truth and transparency are essential not only for individual moral health but for the stability and well-being of the entire community. Corruption, especially when hidden, is seen as a betrayal of both divine and social responsibility.

Christian teachings also echo these themes, emphasizing that true strength lies in living openly and honestly. Jesus warned against hypocrisy, calling for a life of integrity where outward actions align with inner values. In the New Testament, Paul speaks of the importance of "walking in the light" (Ephesians 5:8), living in such a way that one's actions need no concealment. Jesus's admonition that "there is nothing concealed that will not be disclosed" (Luke 12:2) serves as a reminder that, in the end, all hidden acts are brought to light. In the Christian tradition, secretive behavior and hidden corruption are viewed as barriers to spiritual growth, relationships, and authentic community. Transparency is seen as a form of accountability, a way of ensuring that one's life aligns with divine principles of honesty, justice, and love.

Together, these teachings from Islam, Judaism, and Christianity highlight the moral dangers of hidden corruption, reinforcing the idea that true integrity requires transparency and accountability. The Jaredite experience with secret combinations serves as a cautionary tale for us all, warning that when individuals or institutions prioritize secrecy and self-interest, they risk unraveling not only their own integrity but the trust and stability of their communities. Hidden

corruption breeds division, distrust, and ultimately, societal decay—
a pattern as relevant in our time as it was in the Jaredite world.

Reflecting on the impact of secret combinations invites us to
examine our own lives and communities. While few of us may
encounter corruption on the scale of the Jaredite rulers, the
principles remain the same. How often are we tempted to cut
corners, conceal mistakes, or prioritize personal gain over the
common good? Do we act with transparency, even when honesty is
challenging, or do we allow small compromises to erode our
integrity over time? Recognizing these tendencies within ourselves
is the first step in resisting the allure of hidden corruption, both
personally and in the spaces where we lead or influence others.

Taking action to maintain integrity requires vigilance and self-
awareness. We can start by cultivating habits of honesty in our daily
lives—being truthful in our words, transparent in our intentions, and
accountable for our actions. Like the teachings from world religions,
the Jaredite story encourages us to approach life with an open heart,
one that seeks not personal advantage but collective good. By
prioritizing transparency, we not only guard against corruption but
build trust, respect, and a legacy of integrity that positively impacts
everyone around us.

As you reflect on this chapter, consider the areas in your life
where transparency can play a greater role. Are there small

compromises you make that, over time, might weaken your integrity? Are there opportunities to act with honesty and openness, even if doing so requires vulnerability? The Jaredite narrative shows us that integrity is not only a personal virtue but a communal safeguard, one that preserves trust and fosters unity.

In a world where secret combinations still tempt us with promises of easy success or hidden gain, let us choose a path of honesty, integrity, and accountability. By rejecting the allure of hidden corruption, we align ourselves with timeless principles that uplift, strengthen, and unite. By cultivating transparency in our lives, we break the cycle of societal decay, instead creating a foundation of trust and authenticity that sustains both individuals and communities for generations to come.

Summary

As we close Part III, *Leadership Lessons and the Cycles of Faith*, we emerge with a deeper understanding of the tremendous influence leadership has over the course of individuals, families, communities, and even entire civilizations. The Jaredite story, with its highs and lows of faithful kings and prideful rulers, reveals that leadership is more than a role—it is a legacy in the making. Through humble leaders like Orihah, we see the power of humility, service, and integrity to inspire unity and create peace. In the self-serving ambition of leaders like Riplakish, we witness how pride and corruption erode trust, sow discord, and ultimately lead to ruin. Part III calls us to consider: what kind of legacy will our own leadership leave behind?

Leadership, as we have seen, is not a title but a choice, a commitment to lift others up rather than to elevate oneself. The examples in these chapters teach us that true leadership requires a grounding in humility, an openness to serve, and a dedication to transparency. In today's world, these qualities are more important than ever. Whether in our families, workplaces, communities, or places of worship, we are each given opportunities to lead—not through dominance, but through influence, compassion, and integrity. The Jaredite leaders who ruled with humility created lasting peace; those who ruled with pride sparked conflict. These cycles of leadership, repeated over generations, remind us that we, too, are part of a greater cycle, with our actions impacting those who come after us.

The lessons from this section invite us to examine not only how we lead but also how we follow. Do we place our trust in leaders who value transparency and service, or are we drawn to those who promise quick fixes and self-serving gains? In our own lives, do we act with integrity, even in small matters, or do we allow subtle compromises to blur our commitment to truth? Just as the secret combinations in Jaredite society spread like a hidden disease, unchecked pride and small acts of dishonesty can accumulate, ultimately damaging the communities we cherish.

As these chapters have revealed, world religions echo the Jaredite story with calls for humble leadership and ethical stewardship. From the teachings of Jesus on servant leadership to Islamic principles of accountability to Jewish lessons on justice and humility, we see that the path to lasting influence is one paved with values that transcend time and culture. True leadership is marked not by power but by purpose, by a commitment to uphold what is right and to place others' welfare above one's own. The Jaredite leaders who succeeded understood this timeless truth, while those who failed allowed pride to eclipse their duty to serve.

Reflecting on the cycles of faith and pride, we are reminded that each generation, each individual, is called to confront these same choices. Leadership, in its truest sense, is a daily decision to lead by example, to resist the allure of pride, and to prioritize the well-being of others. As we navigate our own leadership roles, let us draw from these stories the courage to lead with humility, the resolve to act with integrity, and the wisdom to remember that our actions resonate far beyond ourselves.

In closing Part III, let us carry forward the lessons of the Jaredite leaders, both the righteous and the fallen, as reminders of the power we each hold to shape our world for better or worse. Let us be leaders who seek to inspire, who act with honesty, and who build communities founded on trust, transparency, and compassion. In choosing this path, we join a legacy of leaders who understand that true greatness is measured not by titles but by the positive impact we leave on the lives around us. As we continue our journey, may we lead with humility, serve with love, and create a cycle of faith that endures for generations.

Author's Reflection

As I look back on Part III, Leadership Lessons and the Cycles of Faith, I find myself considering the weight of influence and the powerful role that leadership—whether intentional or unintentional plays in each of our lives. In the Jaredite story, leaders like Orihah and Riplakish stand as sharp contrasts to one another, their legacies revealing how leadership shapes not only the lives of those who follow, but also the soul of the leader themselves. These stories are not merely historical; they resonate deeply, challenging me to think about how I, too, lead, serve, and affect those around me and the lasting impact I am creating, consciously or not.

The faithful kings in these chapters teach me that humility and service are more than admirable qualities—they are the true foundations of effective leadership. Orihah's reign reminds me that leadership is less about position and more about the commitment to upholding values that foster trust, integrity, and peace. In a world that often prizes influence for the sake of personal gain, Orihah's example is refreshing and humbling, a reminder that the best leaders are often those whose efforts go unsung because they are focused not on elevating themselves but on uplifting others. I am prompted to ask myself: In my relationships, my work, and my community, am I building foundations of trust, or am I seeking recognition? Am I listening as much as I am leading? True leadership, I am beginning to see, requires a constant return to humility and service.

In contrast, the story of Riplakish is a cautionary tale that lingers. His pride, greed, and ruthless ambition echo as a warning, showing me how quickly the desire for control and recognition can corrupt even the noblest intentions. The fall of Riplakish is more than a story of a leader gone wrong—it is a reminder that pride, left unchecked, becomes a cycle of self-destruction, impacting not only the leader but everyone connected to them. As I reflect on his downfall, I am reminded that pride is a subtle adversary; it does not always appear in grandiose displays but can slip in quietly, influencing our decisions in ways that pull us from the path of integrity. The story of Riplakish encourages me to look inward and recognize the quiet, personal battles with pride that each of us faces, prompting me to root out any traces that may cloud my vision and distort my purpose.

The lessons from these Jaredite leaders call me to a higher standard, one that demands self-awareness, integrity, and the courage to lead with humility. I realize that we are all, in our own ways, part of the cycles of faith and pride—cycles that repeat as long as we allow ourselves to be swayed by personal ambition rather than grounded in genuine service. True leadership, as these stories show, is not a single act or title but a continuous choice to act with honor, putting the well-being of others above our own gain. In my own life, I am challenged to examine where I can lead more effectively by serving, to let go of the need for praise, and to focus on creating a legacy built on principles that endure.

The Jaredite stories align with teachings from many traditions, each reminding me that leadership is more than influence; it is a sacred stewardship. In Christianity, Jesus's model of servant leadership, in which the greatest are those who serve, challenges me to look at power not as control but as responsibility. In Islam, the idea of stewardship emphasizes that leadership is ultimately about accountability to something greater than oneself. And in Buddhism, the concept of compassionate authority underscores that leadership should uplift, not suppress, others. Together, these teachings provide a blueprint, guiding me toward leadership that is measured not by success but by the impact I leave on others.

As I step back from Part III, I see that the journey from Babel to Zarahemla is not simply about moving from confusion to clarity, but about transforming how we relate to those around us. This journey challenges me to think critically about how I lead, how I serve, and what I contribute to those who share my path. Each choice I make—whether big or small—either strengthens or weakens the foundations of faith and trust in my life and in the lives of others.

The Jaredite kings' stories inspire me to approach my own leadership roles with greater humility, integrity, and intentionality. They remind me that each act of service, each choice to prioritize others' needs over my own, is a step closer to Zarahemla—a state of peace and unity that I can help create. Moving forward, I carry with me the knowledge that true greatness in leadership lies not in the titles I hold or the recognition I receive but in the quiet legacy of integrity and compassion I leave behind. This is the lesson I take from the Jaredite cycle of faith and pride: that true leadership is not about me but about the difference I make in the lives of others, and that this legacy, built on humility and service, is what ultimately guides me closer to my own promised land.

Part IV

Warnings and Repentance—Lessons from Decline and Redemption

Introduction

A s we enter Part IV, *Warnings and Repentance—Lessons from Decline and Redemption*, we move into one of the most powerful arcs of the Jaredite story—a narrative that showcases both the tragedy of human pride and the relentless mercy of divine grace. Here, we witness the painful consequences of ignoring prophetic warnings as the Jaredites drift further from the principles that once united them. In this section, the Jaredite civilization stands at a crossroads: heed the call to change or face the consequences of unchecked ambition and rebellion. Through their story, we are invited to confront the tension between pride and humility, to consider the power of repentance, and to recognize that, no matter how far we stray, a path to redemption remains open.

The descent of the Jaredite people is not sudden; it is a slow unraveling—a series of choices, each one nudging them further from their values and their connection to God. This pattern of decline is painfully familiar, both in history and in our own lives. The repeated warnings from Ether, who pleads with his people to turn back, echo with urgency, reminding us that decline rarely begins with one momentous act but with small, seemingly insignificant decisions that accumulate over time. The Jaredites' fall serves as a mirror, challenging us to reflect on where we might be ignoring our own "small" warnings, where we might be further drifting from our own values, often without even realizing it.

But as stark as these warnings are, this section is not only a story of decline; it is also of hope. Through the prophet Ether's unyielding message, we see that God's call to repentance is not merely a judgment—it is an invitation to begin again. Over and over, the opportunity to repent and change direction is extended to the Jaredites, illustrating that no matter how deep the descent, redemption is always within reach. This is a message that resonates across faith traditions: in Christianity, the parable of the Prodigal Son reminds us that the door to return is always open. In Buddhism, the idea of *metanoia*—a change of heart—emphasizes that enlightenment is always possible, even after failure. And in Islam, the concept of *tawbah* (repentance) is a continual turning back to Allah, who is "the Most Merciful of those who show mercy."

The story of the Jaredites, then, is both a cautionary tale and a source of hope. It reminds us that while the path of pride and rebellion leads to emptiness, the path of humility and repentance leads to renewal. Just as Ether never gives up on calling his people back to God, we, too, are invited to listen to the subtle nudges in our own lives—the moments that call us to reflect, to realign, and to return to our better selves. This is not a one-time decision but a continual process, a cycle of recognizing our missteps and embracing the grace that allows us to move forward.

As we journey through Part IV, consider the moments in your life where you have felt those gentle (or sometimes not-so-gentle) warnings. Where have you sensed a call to change, to turn around, or to let go of something that may be leading you away from your values? The Jaredite story is a reminder that repentance is not about dwelling in guilt; it is about growth. It is about choosing to move in a direction that brings us closer to God and to the peace that comes from living in alignment with our highest principles.

This section invites us to see the process of repentance not as a burden but as a gift—a chance to rise above the mistakes of the past and to step into a future shaped by humility, integrity, and faith. Just as the Jaredites' journey reaches a critical point, we, too, are reminded that our choices define our path. In choosing to heed the warnings and embrace the opportunity for redemption, we lay the foundation for a life of purpose, peace, and connection to the divine. May Part IV inspire each of us to take an honest look within, recognize the areas where we can realign, and embrace the transformative power of repentance, knowing that each step back to God brings us closer to our own promised land.

The Prophetic Call to Repentance—Listening to Divine Warnings

In Ether 12, we encounter a moment of profound urgency as the prophet Ether pleads with his people to turn back to God. His warnings are not casual; they are calls from a heart burdened by the knowledge of what lies ahead if they continue down their path of pride and rebellion. Moroni, reflecting on Ether's message, expands upon the crucial role of faith in heeding divine warnings, reminding us that faith is not just about believing in promises of prosperity—it is also about trusting in guidance that challenges us, redirects us, and sometimes calls us to make difficult changes. Ether's call to repentance is more than a plea to avoid destruction; it is an invitation to realign with truth, to choose humility over pride, and to rediscover purpose in the midst of spiritual drift.

The urgency of Ether's message echoes throughout the ages, reverberating in the prophetic teachings of Christianity, Judaism, and The Church of Jesus Christ of Latter-day Saints. In each of these traditions, prophets are sent not just to foretell the future but to remind people of the principles that lead to peace, unity, and divine connection. Prophets call us to see beyond the allure of temporary successes, inviting us to make choices that align with eternal truths rather than fleeting desires. Just as Ether calls the Jaredites to turn back, prophets in every era serve as voices of clarity, urging us to pay attention to the consequences of our actions and offering us the path of repentance as a means to avoid unnecessary sorrow.

In Christianity, the call to repentance is central to the teachings of Jesus. In the New Testament, we find examples of Jesus urging people to change course, reminding them that God's kingdom is within reach, but only if they are willing to let go of pride and self-interest. In Matthew 23, Jesus speaks out against hypocrisy and spiritual blindness, calling the Pharisees to recognize their own need for humility. His message is clear: spiritual growth requires an honest examination of our actions and a willingness to make course corrections. Listening to divine warnings is not just about avoiding punishment; it is about embracing transformation and stepping into a fuller, richer life rooted in love and integrity.

Judaism, too, emphasizes the importance of repentance and the power of prophetic counsel. The Hebrew Scriptures are filled with examples of prophets who urged Israel to return to God, to follow the commandments, and to live justly. The prophet Jeremiah's life was devoted to calling the people back from idolatry and injustice, warning them of the impending consequences of their choices. In Jewish tradition, the Days of Awe—the period between Rosh Hashanah and Yom Kippur—are a time of reflection and repentance, a structured reminder to listen to the "still, small voice" that guides us back to our highest values. This period highlights the belief that divine guidance, even when difficult, is a gift—a chance to realign and start anew.

Latter-day Saint teachings similarly emphasize the necessity of heeding prophetic counsel and embracing repentance as an act of faith. Modern-day prophets continue to call members of the Church and all people to repent, to turn from worldly distractions, and to focus on building spiritual resilience. The Book of Mormon itself repeatedly illustrates the "pride cycle," showing how prosperity often leads to complacency, then to pride, and ultimately to a need for repentance. Ether's repeated warnings to the Jaredites are part of this pattern, reminding readers that spiritual health requires constant vigilance and a willingness to course-correct. Prophetic guidance is seen not as a restriction but as a safeguard, helping us navigate the complexities of life with greater wisdom and purpose.

As we explore the calls to repentance found in Ether 12, we are invited to reflect on the prophetic guidance in our own lives. Are there areas where we are ignoring gentle nudges to change, to let go of certain habits, or to make more intentional choices? Prophetic counsel often comes in ways that challenge our comfort zones, pushing us to confront behaviors and attitudes that hold us back from true growth. But these calls are not about condemnation; they are about liberation—freeing us from the limitations of pride, selfishness, and complacency.

Actively listening to divine warnings requires both humility and faith. It means setting aside the defensiveness that often rises when we are confronted with change and opening our hearts to the possibility of transformation. To heed prophetic counsel, we must be willing to trust that God's guidance, even when difficult, is ultimately in our best interest. This involves daily introspection, moments of prayerful self-reflection, and a commitment to act on impressions that prompt us toward change. The more we cultivate this openness, the more we become attuned to the gentle guidance that leads us back to the path of integrity and peace.

As you consider the message of Ether and Moroni, take time to reflect on your own life. Where are you being called to adjust, to shift your focus, or to let go of something that may be holding you back? Listening to prophetic counsel is a practice—a way of living that continually invites us to grow, to let go of pride, and to embrace humility as a pathway to lasting peace. In a world that often celebrates self-reliance and individualism, prophetic guidance reminds us that true strength comes from aligning ourselves with divine truth.

Ultimately, Ether's call to the Jaredites is the same call we receive today: to listen, to reflect, and to repent. The Jaredites' decline serves as a cautionary tale, showing us what happens when warnings are ignored. But it also reminds us that every warning carries within it an opportunity—a chance to begin again, to return to our best selves, and to find peace in God's grace. May we learn from their story, heeding the prophetic call to repentance in our own lives and, in doing so, create a legacy of faith, humility, and resilience as we journey toward our own promised lands.

Coriantumr's Last Stand—The Cost of Unyielding Pride

In Ether 13–15, the story of Coriantumr reaches its tragic climax, one that serves as a powerful reminder of the costs of unyielding pride. Coriantumr's resistance to repentance becomes not just his personal downfall but the downfall of his entire people. Warned repeatedly by the prophet Ether to turn back, to let go of pride, and to seek peace, Coriantumr instead clings stubbornly to his power and his ambition. The result is a spiral of devastation—a cycle of violence, loss, and destruction that consumes not only Coriantumr but also everyone around him. His story stands as a sobering testament to what happens when pride blinds us to the need for change, locking us in patterns that lead only to suffering and regret.

Coriantumr's story is not simply one of defeat in battle; it is a deeper tragedy of resistance to growth, of ignoring repeated opportunities for repentance. His refusal to let go of pride traps him in a cycle of conflict, demonstrating a fundamental truth found across spiritual traditions: unchecked pride and ego lead to suffering, not fulfillment. In Buddhist and Hindu teachings, this is the essence of karma—the idea that our actions, driven by intentions, create cycles of cause and effect that shape our lives and the lives of others. Prideful actions sow seeds of conflict and division, setting into motion forces that inevitably come back to us, often with devastating consequences. Coriantumr's refusal to repent is not just a personal flaw; it is a catalyst that sets in motion a karmic cycle from which he cannot escape.

In Buddhism, the concept of *tanha* (craving or attachment) explains how unbridled desires and clinging to self-image are sources of suffering. Buddha taught that attachment to ego, and a desire for control keep individuals trapped in a cycle of *samsara*, or continuous rebirth, marked by suffering and dissatisfaction. Pride, in this sense, is a form of attachment to the self—a refusal to let go of one's image, status, or power, even when it leads to harm. In Coriantumr's story, we see this attachment to his position as king and his reluctance to yield, even in the face of impending destruction. Like the Buddhist caution against attachment, his resistance ultimately keeps him bound in a cycle that erodes his chances for peace and connection.

Hindu philosophy also speaks to the consequences of unyielding pride through the concept of *karma*, where every action has a corresponding reaction. The Bhagavad Gita discusses the importance of performing actions with humility, detachment, and a focus on a higher purpose. Leaders, especially, are encouraged to act with *dharma* (duty) rather than with ego, as selfish motivations lead to destructive outcomes. Coriantumr's story is a caution against failing to recognize this cycle of cause and effect, highlighting the inevitability of consequences when one's actions are driven by pride and resistance. In the end, his refusal to humble himself before Ether's prophetic warnings creates a karmic cycle that brings suffering not only to himself but to his entire people—a tragic outcome that could have been avoided with a single act of humility.

The lesson from Coriantumr's last stand is one that transcends time and culture: pride can be an impenetrable wall, blocking us from change, growth, and ultimately, peace. His story invites us to look inward and ask ourselves where we might be resisting necessary changes in our own lives. Are there areas where pride is holding us back, where we cling to self-image or ambition at the expense of our well-being or relationships? Are there times when we, like Coriantumr, hear the call to change but resist it, unwilling to let go of control or power? His story serves as a mirror, urging us to examine our own hearts and identify where pride may be leading us down paths of needless struggle.

The power of Coriantumr's story lies not only in its tragedy but in the warning it offers. Each of us has the opportunity to break the cycles of pride, to recognize the moments when we are invited to change and to choose humility over resistance. This does not mean surrendering our goals or values; it means letting go of the ego that insists on being right, that refuses to yield, and that would rather suffer than grow. Choosing humility, in Coriantumr's case, could have saved lives, avoided wars, and brought peace to his people. In our own lives, choosing humility can open the door to healthier relationships, personal growth, and a clearer path to inner peace.

Reflect on Coriantumr's story and consider areas in your own life where pride might be limiting you. Is there a call to change—a subtle nudge to let go of something—that you have been resisting? Are there relationships or situations where humility could transform conflict into connection? In choosing to let go of pride, we allow ourselves to break free from cycles of frustration, resentment, and isolation. We embrace the wisdom of releasing attachment to self-image, recognizing that true strength comes from the ability to change, to grow, and to respond to life with openness rather than rigidity.

Ultimately, Coriantumr's story reminds us that the cost of unyielding pride is far greater than the price of humility. While pride insists on maintaining control, humility opens doors to possibilities that pride cannot foresee. By learning from Coriantumr's experience, we gain insight into the value of listening to warnings, embracing humility, and choosing a path that leads not to cycles of conflict but to cycles of peace and renewal.

As we consider Coriantumr's last stand, let us take his story as a call to action in our own lives. May we be willing to recognize and release the pride that keeps us from changing, heed the gentle (or sometimes forceful) warnings in our lives, and find the courage to choose humility over resistance. In doing so, we avoid the needless suffering that comes from clinging to our own way, and we step instead into a path of growth, connection, and peace—moving ever closer to our own promised lands.

Summary

As we reach the conclusion of Part IV, *Warnings and Repentance—Lessons from Decline and Redemption*, the Jaredite story leaves us with a powerful and enduring message: while the path of pride and resistance leads to sorrow, the path of humility and repentance brings hope, growth, and the possibility of renewal. The decline of the Jaredite civilization is a cautionary tale, showing us the high costs of ignoring divine warnings and clinging to self-serving ambitions. But amid the tragedy, there is also a message of profound grace—the reminder that repentance, even when delayed, is always within reach and that redemption is never out of our grasp if we are willing to change.

Ether's prophetic calls to his people are not simply words of judgment; they are invitations to course-correct and to realign with the principles of peace, humility, and unity. His warnings are echoes of the loving persistence that we find in our own lives—those moments when life nudges us toward reflection, inviting us to assess our direction and make the adjustments needed to avoid needless suffering. The Jaredite story reveals that while we are free to make our own choices, we are never beyond the reach of divine grace, a grace that continually offers us the opportunity to begin again.

The themes of warning and repentance resonate across spiritual traditions, reminding us that change is always possible, even after moments of failure. In Christianity, the parable of the Prodigal Son speaks to the joy and relief found in returning to our spiritual center, where we are met with compassion rather than condemnation. In Buddhism, the concept of *metanoia*—a change of heart or mind—emphasizes that enlightenment often comes through acknowledging our own missteps and choosing a different path. In Islam, the idea of *tawbah*, or turning back to God, teaches that there is no sin too great to be forgiven and that every step toward repentance is a step back to peace. Together, these teachings affirm that the journey of repentance is not a punishment; it is an act of love, a chance to rewrite our story with wisdom and grace.

As Elder D. Todd Christofferson so beautifully stated, "May we bury—very, very deep—any element of rebellion against God in our lives and replace it with a willing heart and a willing mind." This is not an act of surrender but of liberation, freeing ourselves from the burdens that weigh us down and opening our hearts to divine transformation.

He further reminds us that "burying our weapons of rebellion against God simply means yielding to the enticing of the Holy Spirit, putting off the natural man, and becoming 'a saint through the atonement of Christ the Lord.'"

The story of Coriantumr and the final days of the Jaredites remind us that the consequences of pride and resistance can be severe, but they also illuminate the transformative power of humility. In Coriantumr's last stand, we see the high cost of ignoring opportunities to change. His refusal to heed warnings leads him to a place of isolation and loss. Yet even in his final moments, there is a glimmer of awareness—a realization, perhaps, that humility could have brought peace instead of destruction. His story urges us to consider the moments in our own lives when pride or fear may be holding us back from growth, inviting us to step out of the cycles of resistance and into a path of connection and purpose.

As we close this section, let us carry forward the lessons of warning and repentance into our own lives. Are there areas where we need to heed gentle (or even urgent) calls for change? Are there patterns of behavior, habits, or attitudes that no longer serve us that may be leading us away from peace and fulfillment? In reflecting on the Jaredite journey, we are reminded that while life's challenges and setbacks are inevitable, how we respond to them defines our path. Choosing to heed divine guidance and embracing repentance allows us to rise above our mistakes to find healing and transformation in places where we might otherwise find regret.

The journey from Babel to Zarahemla is, at its core, a journey of becoming—of recognizing our own tendencies toward pride and self-interest and learning to replace them with humility, openness, and a willingness to change. The Jaredites' story is both a warning and a gift, offering us insights that empower us to avoid their fate and to seek our own "promised lands" through choices rooted in integrity, courage, and faith. As we continue forward, may we carry with us the knowledge that redemption is always possible, that no moment is beyond the reach of grace, and that every decision to change is a step closer to peace, purpose, and divine connection.

Author's Reflection

As I reflect on Part IV, Warnings and Repentance—Lessons from Decline and Redemption, I am struck by the Jaredite story's depth and relevance in my own life. Their journey isn't just about the rise and fall of a civilization—it's a story that echoes the very human struggle between pride and humility, resistance and repentance. In the slow unraveling of the Jaredite people, I see a pattern familiar to us all: the tendency to overlook small warnings, to resist change when it feels uncomfortable, and to ignore the subtle nudges that urge us to take a different path. Each time I read Ether's pleas, I recognize the weight of choices made without reflection, of opportunities lost due to pride or stubbornness. This part of the journey reminds me that, like the Jaredites, I am also constantly at a crossroads, choosing either to ignore these calls for change or to let them guide me toward growth and peace.

The Jaredites' decline does not happen immediately. It is a gradual drift, a series of small decisions that eventually lead them away from what they once held dear. I see this in myself, too. How often do I convince myself that minor mistakes do not matter, that I can course-correct later? Yet Ether's warnings reveal a deeper truth: when left unchecked, even the smallest choices can lead us far from where we intended to go. Repentance, then, becomes not a punishment but an invitation—a way to turn back, realign, and find the path I may have strayed from. It is a reminder that humility, though difficult, is the gateway to peace and connection, not only with others but with my best self.

As I consider the importance of repentance, I am reminded of teachings from other faiths that echo Ether's call to course-correct. In Christianity, the parable of the Prodigal Son has always resonated with me. His journey back to his father—marked by humility and the willingness to change—illustrates that no matter how far I may wander, the path back is always open. In Buddhism, the concept of metanoia, or a change of heart, offers a similar insight: the moment I recognize my missteps and choose to alter my course, I find clarity and renewed purpose. And in Islam, the idea of tawbah, or turning back to God, reinforces that even the smallest steps toward repentance bring me closer to peace. Each of these traditions reminds me that repentance is not about guilt; it is about renewal, a process of becoming more aligned with my values and aspirations.

In the figure of Coriantumr, I find a powerful warning. His story is the cautionary tale of what happens when pride overrides humility when fear of losing power blinds us to the chance for redemption. As I consider Coriantumr's resistance, I am compelled to ask myself: Where does pride hold me back from making necessary changes? Are there areas in my life where I am clinging to control, even when it prevents me from moving forward? Coriantumr's last stand is a stark reminder that refusing to yield, to let go, to seek a different path leads to isolation and regret. His fate pushes me to examine my own choices and recognize that humility and repentance are not weaknesses—they are acts of courage that lead me to a more meaningful, connected life.

Part IV has reminded me that the journey from Babel to Zarahemla is as much an internal journey as it is a physical one. It is a process of shedding pride, letting go of resistance, and embracing the chance to begin again. In the story of the Jaredites, I find both a caution and a comfort—a reminder that while ignoring warnings leads to pain, heeding them brings peace. I see that every time I choose humility over pride, reflection over resistance, I am taking a step closer to my own "promised land." Repentance becomes not only a way to avoid decline but a path toward growth, resilience, and greater alignment with the values I hold most dear.

As I move forward, I am more mindful of the warnings in my life, those subtle signs that encourage me to change course, to let go of habits or mindsets that no longer serve me. The story of the Jaredites inspires me to approach these moments with a spirit of humility, to see them as opportunities for transformation rather than obstacles to avoid. This part of the Jaredite journey teaches me that while pride may offer a fleeting sense of power, only humility leads to lasting peace. The road to Zarahemla, it turns out, is paved not with perfection but with the willingness to listen, to change, and to return, over and over again, to the path that brings me closer to my true self.

Part V

Gathering the Pieces—
Applying Jaredite and
Global Wisdom Today

Introduction

As we step into Part V, *Gathering the Pieces—Applying Jaredite and Global Wisdom Today*, we move from reflection to action, from ancient narrative to personal application. Here, the Jaredite journey becomes more than a historical or symbolic tale—it becomes a guide for our lives, a source of practical wisdom we can apply in today's complex world. This section is about gathering the lessons we have encountered along the Jaredite path and weaving them into our daily choices, our relationships, and our spiritual journeys. The story of the Jaredites, enriched by insights from world religions, invites us to ask: How can these timeless principles help us navigate our challenges, seek peace, and become leaders in our own right?

The Jaredite experience holds up a mirror to humanity's deepest questions—questions about humility and pride, strength and vulnerability, connection and isolation. In their journey from Babel to their own promised land, the Jaredites faced trials that are remarkably familiar: the need to exercise faith amidst uncertainty, the challenge of building resilience through preparation, the dangers of pride and hidden agendas, and the power of humility and repentance. Each episode from their story is a reminder that the spiritual path is not a straight line but a series of choices, each one guiding us closer to—or further from—the lives we want to lead.

This is where the Jaredite wisdom merges with global teachings, showing us that no matter our background or beliefs, the path to peace and purpose follows universal principles that speak to the soul.

As we bring together the insights from the Jaredite story, we are also drawing upon the wealth of wisdom from other traditions. In Christianity, we learn about servant leadership and the importance of humility from the teachings of Jesus, who taught that true greatness is found in serving others. From Buddhism, we understand the value of inner reflection and the need to transcend ego-driven desires to achieve clarity and compassion. In Islam, the concept of stewardship reminds us that our lives and resources are responsibilities to be managed with integrity and generosity. Hinduism offers insights into the principle of *dharma*, encouraging us to act with purpose, honor, and a commitment to the greater good. These principles, threaded through the Jaredite journey, remind us that the quest for truth, peace, and divine connection is universal, transcending time, culture, and religion.

This section, then, is an invitation to employ these lessons actively. The Jaredite story asks us to look at our own lives and ask: Are we acting upon the guidance we receive? Are we leading with humility? Are we building the foundations of faith and integrity that will sustain us through life's "great deeps"? In applying these principles, we are not simply observing a story; we are engaging with it, letting its lessons shape who we are and how we choose to live. Just as the Jaredites faced their moments of decision, we too encounter crossroads—choices that will determine the course of our personal and spiritual journeys.

Let Part V be a call to action, a challenge to take the wisdom of the Jaredites and make it relevant, alive, and actionable. May we gather the pieces, recognizing that while our journeys may differ in detail, the lessons we need are universal. Whether we are building faith, seeking humility, or embracing the courage to change, the Jaredite path shows us that true spiritual growth is about gathering the fragments of wisdom we encounter, piecing them together, and letting them guide us toward the peace, purpose, and connection we seek. As we move forward, may we carry these insights with us, weaving them into a life that honors the past, enriches the present, and prepares us for the future. The journey from Babel to Zarahemla may have been theirs, but the journey to our own "promised lands" is ours to embrace.

Faith and Revelation—Seeking Divine Light and Guidance

The brother of Jared's journey is one of remarkable faith, a path that leads him to a revelation so powerful it transcends his understanding of God and creation. Faced with the daunting task of crossing the "great deep" with his people, the brother of Jared does not merely wait for guidance; he seeks it with unwavering resolve, even daring to ask God to touch stones to give light for their journey. This act of profound faith opens the door to one of the most intimate encounters with the Divine in scripture—an experience that reveals not only God's power but His personal presence, His willingness to be known by those who sincerely seek Him. In this extraordinary moment, the brother of Jared shows us that revelation is not accidental; it is the natural outgrowth of a faith that actively seeks, trusts, and believes.

The story of the brother of Jared serves as a model of faith-driven revelation, illustrating that divine guidance is available to those who pursue it wholeheartedly. His faith is more than belief—it's a commitment, a choice to act even without knowing the outcome, trusting that light will be given as it is needed. His approach to faith is not passive; it is deeply engaged, requiring him to take steps forward, to ask, and to trust that God will respond. In doing so, he shows us that revelation is not a distant or mysterious occurrence reserved for a select few; it is an invitation extended to each of us, a pathway open to anyone willing to seek, ask, and listen.

Across religious traditions, we find a similar call to seeking divine light and guidance. In Christianity, Jesus invites His followers to "ask, and it shall be given you; seek, and ye shall find; knock, and it shall be opened unto you" (Matthew 7:7). This promise speaks to the core of Christian faith: that God is a loving Father who desires to guide His children and who responds to sincere seekers. For Christians, faith is not just belief; it is an active relationship with God, one that involves continually seeking His will and being open to His answers, even when they come in unexpected ways. This approach mirrors the brother of Jared's experience, reminding us that revelation often requires both the courage to ask and the openness to receive.

In Latter-day Saint teachings, personal revelation is central to the faith journey. The principle of "line upon line, precept upon precept" suggests that guidance is given incrementally as we act on what we know and remain receptive to further light. This concept encourages believers to engage in daily practices of prayer, scripture study, and reflection, fostering a living relationship with God that is continually renewed and deepened. Like the brother of Jared, Latter-day Saints are taught to approach God with faith and expectancy, trusting that answers will come in ways that are both timely and transformative. Revelation, in this context, is not a one-time event but a lifelong process, a continuous unfolding of divine insight that shapes every step of the journey.

In Hinduism and Buddhism, the pursuit of wisdom and understanding is seen as a gradual process, one that involves deep reflection and a surrender of ego. In Hindu philosophy, seeking divine guidance often involves meditation, prayer, and acts of devotion that align the heart and mind with the divine will. The

Bhagavad Gita speaks of *shraddha* (faith) as a vital quality, urging seekers to trust that spiritual insight will come to those who seek it sincerely. In Buddhism, the path to enlightenment involves shedding attachments and cultivating awareness, allowing the mind to become open to truth. Both traditions emphasize that revelation—or spiritual insight—is a journey, one that requires patience, humility, and a willingness to let go of preconceived notions.

Together, these traditions remind us that seeking divine guidance is not about demanding answers; it is about cultivating a posture of openness, humility, and faith that invites wisdom into our lives. Like the brother of Jared, we are encouraged to approach God not with rigid expectations but with a willingness to be led, to accept guidance as it comes, and to trust in the process even when the outcome is unclear. Faith, in this sense, is not merely a belief in something unseen; it is an active, ongoing relationship with the Divine, a daily practice of seeking light and listening for answers.

As we reflect on the brother of Jared's story and these teachings from across spiritual traditions, we are invited to consider our own approach to faith and revelation. Are we seeking God's guidance with the same fervor and the same trust that light will come as it is needed? Do we approach God with an openness to receive, even if the answers may challenge us or lead us in unexpected directions? Faith-driven revelation requires us to put aside our need for control, to let go of the fear that may hold us back, and to believe that God's answers—no matter when or how they come—will bring us closer to truth, peace, and purpose.

To make faith an active part of our lives, we can begin by creating daily practices that foster this openness to divine light. Whether through prayer, meditation, journaling, or quiet reflection, these moments help us attune ourselves to God's voice, making us more receptive to the insights and guidance that may come. Revelation, like light, is often subtle, appearing in moments of stillness and clarity. By prioritizing time to listen and seek, we align ourselves with God's timing, trusting that the answers we need will come when we are ready to receive them.

The story of the brother of Jared teaches us that faith is more than belief; it is a journey of trust, an invitation to connect with the divine in ways that illuminate our path. As we seek our own "stones of light," may we do so with the courage to ask, the patience to wait, and the openness to see God's hand in our lives, guiding us ever closer to our own promised lands. Faith-driven revelation is not a destination; it is an unfolding process, a journey that brings us into deeper alignment with God and with the light that guides us all.

Hope and Humility—Lessons from Righteous Leadership and Prophets

In the story of the Jaredites, we encounter figures who exemplify hope and humility as more than just virtues—they are lifelines that carry them through the peaks and valleys of life's most challenging moments. Kings like Orihah and prophets like Ether reveal that humility is not about weakness; it is a quiet strength that allows us to face life's uncertainties with courage and grace. Orihah's leadership, marked by humility and dedication to his people, brought peace and prosperity, while Ether's resilience and hope in the face of rejection and societal decline taught the Jaredites (and us) the power of staying anchored in faith, even when the world seems to crumble around us. Their examples are reminders that hope and humility are not passive traits—they are active forces that ground us, guiding us through whatever trials we face.

Orihah's reign stands out in the Jaredite history for its balance, peace, and stability. His strength lay not in dominating or seeking recognition but in leading with humility, focusing on the well-being of his people over his own pride. His approach to leadership mirrors what many religious traditions describe as the essence of righteous governance: a commitment to service and the courage to lead without ego. For Orihah, humility was not about downplaying his role as king; it was about understanding that his role was not for self-glorification but for the benefit of those he served. His legacy reminds us that humility is not thinking less of ourselves but thinking of ourselves less, creating room for us to uplift and inspire others.

In contrast, Ether's story is one of resilience and unwavering hope. As a prophet, he lived during the Jaredites' darkest days, persistently calling his people to repentance even as they rejected him and descended into chaos. Despite the repeated rejection of his message, Ether's hope never wavered, rooted in his belief that God's promises would ultimately prevail. His resilience illustrates that hope is not merely dreaming; it is a deep-seated trust that sustains us through difficult times, empowering us to move forward even when the outcome is uncertain. Through Ether, we learn that hope paired with humility gives us the strength to endure, to keep striving, and to trust that there is a purpose beyond what we can immediately see.

World religions emphasize these qualities of humility and resilience as foundational to spiritual strength, recognizing them as anchors in the journey of faith. In Buddhism, humility is seen as a means of reducing ego and fostering compassion for others. By setting aside self-centered desires, practitioners open themselves to greater understanding and connection. The Buddhist practice of *mindfulness* cultivates humility by helping individuals let go of attachments to self-image, encouraging a focus on the present moment rather than the endless pursuit of recognition. This approach reflects Ether's focus on his divine calling rather than on his popularity, illustrating that humility is not about seeking validation but about serving with purpose and grace.

In Christianity, Jesus exemplifies the power of humility, teaching that "the greatest among you shall be your servant" (Matthew 23:11). His life was one of service, demonstrating that true strength lies in lifting others and putting their needs above our own. Christian teachings remind us that humility is not weakness; it is the foundation of love, compassion, and community. Ether's dedication to his mission, despite his people's resistance, mirrors this principle of servant leadership. His commitment to his prophetic calling, regardless of his personal comfort or success, echoes Jesus's example of humble service and reminds us that true leadership is grounded in the courage to serve.

In Islam, the concept of *sabr* (patience and perseverance) highlights the importance of enduring life's challenges with hope and humility. Believers are encouraged to trust in Allah's timing and to approach hardships with a heart willing to accept what they cannot control. The Quran says, "And be patient. Indeed, Allah is with the patient" (Quran 8:46), emphasizing that resilience and faith are intertwined. This perspective aligns with Ether's experience; his hope was not rooted in immediate results but in a patient trust that his work would matter, even if he didn't see the fruits himself. His story resonates as a reminder that patience and hope sustain us, especially when our circumstances seem insurmountable.

In Hinduism, the concept of *dharma*—one's duty or path— often requires humility and resilience, as it involves accepting one's role in the larger cosmic order. The Bhagavad Gita teaches that fulfilling one's duty with humility, detached from personal glory, aligns the individual with a higher purpose. Ether's commitment to his prophetic duty, regardless of the opposition he faced, illustrates this principle, showing us that humility and resilience are essential for living a life aligned with divine purpose. In following his dharma, Ether teaches us that hope is not just about anticipating a favorable outcome; it is about faithfully walking our path and trusting in the purpose that guides us.

So how can we cultivate this hope and humility in our own lives, especially when faced with life's uncertainties? Here are a few practical exercises:

1. **Daily Reflection**: Spend a few moments each day reflecting on the ways you can bring humility into your interactions. Ask yourself: Where can I listen more deeply, offer support without seeking recognition, or place the needs of others above my own? Reflection builds awareness, helping us recognize pride or ego in subtle ways and replace it with an attitude of service.

2. **Practicing Gratitude**: Humility often begins with gratitude. Make a habit of writing down three things you are grateful for each day, focusing not only on accomplishments but also on the small blessings and the people who make a difference

in your life. Recognizing that much of what we have comes from others helps us cultivate humility and appreciate our place in a larger community.

3. **Setting Intentions for Service**: Each morning, set an intention to help or uplift someone during the day, whether through a kind word, a helping hand, or simply listening. Like Orihah, lead by example and focus on others' well-being. These simple acts reinforce the idea that leadership is about serving and connecting, helping us build a foundation of humble and compassionate leadership.

4. **Building Resilience through Faith**: When facing challenges, remind yourself of Ether's hope and patience. Write down moments in the past when resilience has helped you overcome difficulties. Reflecting on these experiences can anchor you in hope, reminding you that each trial is an opportunity to grow and strengthen your trust in the process.

5. **Mindful Letting Go**: Practice releasing your attachment to specific outcomes by engaging in mindfulness exercises, such as deep breathing or guided meditation. Focus on letting go of control and accepting that some things are beyond your reach. This exercise builds the humility to accept life's uncertainties and allows hope to flourish even in the face of unknowns.

Orihah and Ether's stories remind us that hope and humility are not abstract ideals; they are choices we make daily. By integrating these qualities into our lives, we anchor ourselves in a faith that endures, regardless of the circumstances. As we cultivate humility, we open ourselves to deeper connections with others, recognizing our shared journey. And as we nurture hope, we build resilience that carries us through challenges, allowing us to see beyond present difficulties to the possibilities that lie ahead.

As you embrace these lessons from Orihah and Ether, remember that hope and humility are not destinations but practices, pathways that guide us toward a life of meaning, service, and peace. In a world that often rewards self

Bearing Witness—Living as Examples of Faith and Integrity

As the final witness to the rise and fall of the Jaredite civilization, Moroni stands as a singular figure—a lone voice committed to preserving the story, bearing testimony to the lessons learned, and urging future generations to heed its warnings. Moroni's role as a witness is more than historical record-keeping; it is a testament to the power of faith and integrity, a legacy left not only in words but in the commitment to truth that defines his every action. Through Moroni's example, we are reminded that bearing witness is not merely a matter of recounting facts; it is a way of living with integrity, of showing through our actions what we genuinely believe. His final witness, shaped by resilience and faith, calls us to ask ourselves: How can we be witnesses in our own lives? How can our actions, our words, and our presence testify to the truths we hold most dearly?

Moroni's commitment to the Jaredite record embodies the concept of personal testimony as a "living witness." His example invites us to see our own lives as opportunities to reflect our deepest values, our own journeys of faith, and our experiences with God. This type of witness goes beyond spoken words; it becomes visible in the way we treat others, in the choices we make, and in the principles we uphold, even when no one else is watching. Bearing witness is not about perfection; it is about authenticity. It is about being honest in our convictions and letting our lives reflect the integrity, faith, and resilience we wish to see in the world.

In Christianity, bearing witness is foundational. Jesus teaches His followers to "let your light so shine before others, that they may see your good deeds and glorify your Father in heaven" (Matthew 5:16). This light—our faith, our hope, our love—becomes a testimony in itself, a visible sign of God's presence in our lives. The Christian call to bear witness is not confined to words; it is an invitation to live in a way that inspires others to seek truth and connection. Whether through acts of kindness, courage in the face of adversity, or integrity in small matters, Christians are called to reflect Christ's love and truth in everything they do. This mirrors Moroni's dedication to his witness, showing us that testimony is as much about how we live as it is about what we say.

In Judaism, the concept of *kedushah*, or holiness, emphasizes that each person's actions can sanctify the world, bearing witness to God's covenant. Jewish teachings encourage believers to embody *tikkun olam*—the responsibility to "repair the world" through acts of justice, kindness, and integrity. Living as a witness in Judaism means honoring God not only in prayer but in everyday actions that reflect commitment to truth, compassion, and community. Moroni's commitment to preserving the Jaredite story aligns with this principle, as he seeks to bear witness to the lessons that might guide future generations toward unity, justice, and peace.

In Islam, the concept of *shahada*, or bearing witness, is central to the faith. The *Shahada*, the declaration that "there is no god but Allah, and Muhammad is His Messenger," is more than a statement; it is a daily commitment to live with integrity, aligning one's life with God's will. Islamic teachings encourage believers to be *shahid*, or witnesses, through their actions, embodying the virtues of honesty, compassion, and accountability. Moroni's unwavering dedication to his task resonates with this idea of a living witness, showing that to truly testify to one's faith, one must live it out with consistency, even when circumstances make it difficult.

Buddhism, too, offers insights into bearing witness through the concept of *sangha*, or spiritual community, where individuals support each other on the path to enlightenment. Buddhists bear witness to truth by cultivating mindfulness, compassion, and non-attachment, letting their actions speak to their commitment to inner peace and harmony. The life of a Buddhist witness is one that radiates calm, resilience, and a dedication to truth. In this way, Moroni's solitary witness resembles the example of the *bodhisattva*—a being who endures and sacrifices for the benefit of others, preserving wisdom that can guide future seekers toward a life of meaning.

Together, these perspectives highlight the universal call to bear witness, reminding us that our testimonies are most powerful when they are lived. Moroni's example challenges us to embody our beliefs, to let our actions reflect our convictions, and to become living examples of the faith and integrity we hope to inspire in others. Bearing witness is not about grand gestures; it is about showing up daily with honesty, humility, and kindness. It is about letting the small, consistent actions of our lives speak to our faith, our values, and our commitment to truth.

So, how can we bear witness in our own lives? Here are a few ways to let your life be a testimony of what you believe:

1. **Practice Consistency**: Integrity shines brightly in the small, everyday decisions. Aim to act consistently with your values, whether in private or in public. Moroni's life teaches us that a witness rooted in integrity does not change based on circumstance; it holds steady, a reliable source of light and truth for others.

2. **Embrace Vulnerability**: Testimony is not about presenting a perfect image. Share your challenges and growth with others. By being open about our struggles, we create connections, allowing others to see that faith and resilience are built through real, imperfect experiences. Bearing witness is about showing how we grow and learn, not about pretending we have it all figured out.

3. **Serve with Compassion**: Actions speak louder than words. Acts of kindness, especially when they are unseen, become a living testimony of the values we hold. Serve those around you, offer a listening ear, and look for ways to support others on their journeys. Compassionate service speaks to the heart, bearing witness to the love, empathy, and interconnectedness that binds us all.

4. **Reflect Your Faith in Challenges**: Moroni's role as the final witness was not easy; he faced isolation, uncertainty, and loss. In our own lives, we bear witness by holding to hope,

resilience, and trust even in difficult times. Letting our faith guide us through challenges speaks volumes, inspiring others to see that faith is not just for good times but a source of strength through adversity.

5. **Live with Purpose**: Bearing witness is about aligning our lives with a purpose that reaches beyond ourselves. By dedicating ourselves to something greater—whether through service, creativity, or teaching—we become channels for wisdom, compassion, and connection. Moroni's witness was not just for himself; it was a gift for future generations. Living with purpose allows our lives to echo with meaning, inspiring others to find their own path.

As we strive to bear witness in our lives, let Moroni's example remind us that our actions, big and small, contribute to a legacy of faith, integrity, and hope. Each act of kindness, each choice made with honesty, and each moment spent in service becomes part of the story we are telling the world about what we believe. In bearing witness, we become more than followers of faith; we become sources of light, reminders of resilience, and examples of the power of living with purpose and conviction.

May we all be witnesses in our lives, reflecting the values and truths we hold dear, letting our lives serve as quiet but powerful testaments to faith, integrity, and love. In doing so, we honor

Moroni's legacy and carry forward the timeless truth that living with purpose, honesty, and compassion is the most profound testimony we can offer.

Summary

As we conclude Part V, *Gathering the Pieces—Applying Jaredite and Global Wisdom Today*, we stand with a clearer sense of how the Jaredite story can inform and enrich our own lives. From the humble leadership of Orihah to the relentless hope of Ether, and from the tragic pride of Coriantumr to the unshakable faith of the brother of Jared, the Jaredite narrative offers wisdom that is both timeless and deeply relevant. These stories are no longer just ancient accounts of rise and fall; they are reflections of our own journeys, full of moments that call for courage, humility, resilience, and trust in a greater purpose.

In this section, we have pieced together the Jaredite lessons with insights from world traditions, discovering that while cultures and beliefs may differ, the spiritual truths that guide us are universal. From the Christian call to be a light to Buddhist mindfulness to Islamic stewardship and Jewish dedication to justice, we see that each tradition brings a unique lens to our shared search for truth, peace, and meaning. These teachings, woven into the Jaredite story, reveal that faith, humility, and resilience are not only virtues but also tools for navigating life's complexities with grace and integrity.

But the journey does not end here. As we gather these lessons, the true challenge begins: How will we live them? How will we apply the principles of hope, humility, and integrity in our own lives, workplaces, families, and communities? The Jaredite story is a call to action, inviting us to become more than observers of wisdom—to become participants, living examples of faith and growth. Employing these lessons is an ongoing journey, one that asks us to pause, reflect, and respond with intention, allowing each decision to be guided by principles that uplift us and those around us.

The Jaredite story also reminds us that life is full of crossroads—moments when we can choose to embrace growth, to release pride, to seek forgiveness, or to lead with love. These choices shape not only our lives but the legacy we leave behind. Like Moroni, who bore witness to the Jaredite story so that others might learn and grow, we too, are creating our own stories, writing our own chapters with each decision we make. The wisdom we have gathered is not meant to be kept; it is meant to be shared through our actions, our examples, and the lives we touch.

As we step forward, may we carry these pieces of wisdom with us as guides and companions on our journey. Let us lead with humility, rooted in the knowledge that true greatness lies in service. Let us approach each day with hope, trusting that every challenge is an opportunity for growth and that light will always find a way through the darkness. Let us embrace faith as a living, breathing relationship, one that keeps us open to guidance, resilience, and the quiet strength that comes from aligning ourselves with a purpose beyond ourselves.

The Jaredite journey from Babel to their own promised land mirrors our own journey toward peace, understanding, and spiritual connection. Their story is both a mirror and a map, reflecting our own strengths and weaknesses, our trials and triumphs, while also guiding us to become our best selves. As we gather these pieces of wisdom, let us remember that we, too, are part of a larger story, one that spans generations, cultures, and faiths. The wisdom we choose to live becomes part of that story, shaping not only our lives but also the lives of those who follow.

In closing, may we honor the Jaredite legacy by living with purpose, compassion, and integrity. May we carry these insights forward, letting them shape our choices and actions, creating lives that reflect the wisdom we have gathered and the faith that sustains us. And as we continue our own journey, may we find the courage, humility, and hope to move ever closer to our own "promised lands," trusting that with each step, we are part of something beautiful, meaningful, and eternally worthwhile.

Author's Reflection

As I reflect on Part V, Gathering the Pieces—Applying Jaredite and Global Wisdom Today, I feel both a sense of completion and a call to new beginnings. The Jaredite journey, which started in the confusion of Babel and ended in the desolate echoes of their final wars, holds a mirror to our own lives, showing us that spiritual growth is never a straight line but a series of choices that bring us closer to—or further from—our deepest values. This final section brings the wisdom of the Jaredites into focus, reminding me that the challenge is not in understanding these lessons but in living them, in letting them shape who I am, how I treat others, and how I respond to life's inevitable trials.

The Jaredite story feels especially powerful because, at its core, it is a story of becoming. Orihah's humble leadership, the brother of Jared's daring faith, Ether's enduring hope, and even Coriantumr's final reckoning with pride all speak to the transformative journey that each of us is on. Each of these figures represents qualities I aspire to develop—humility, resilience, courage, and integrity—but they also remind me that these virtues are not goals to reach for the last time. They are qualities I must actively cultivate each day, especially in moments when they do not come easily.

Exploring the Jaredite story alongside the wisdom of other faiths has expanded my understanding of what it means to live a life grounded in purpose and connection. Christianity's call to "let your light shine" challenges me to see my life as a form of witness, an opportunity to reflect kindness, faith, and integrity in ways that inspire others. Buddhism's emphasis on mindfulness and non-attachment reminds me to focus on the present, letting go of pride and ego to find peace in simply being. Islam's concept of shahada, or bearing witness, and Judaism's call to tikkun olam, or repairing the world, push me to see that my life is part of a larger story, one that involves a commitment not just to myself but to the well-being of others.

As I gather these insights, I realize that they all point to a life of integrity and intentionality. The Jaredite story, with its cycles of faith, pride, repentance, and redemption, is a reminder that we are constantly choosing the paths that define us. The journey from Babel to Zarahemla, for me, has come to represent the journey from confusion to clarity, from self-interest to community, and from pride to humility. The wisdom I have gathered is not about avoiding mistakes or living perfectly; it is about embracing the process, learning from each step, and being willing to turn back and begin again whenever needed.

In my own life, I see how easy it is to drift, to let the busyness of daily demands drown out the quiet calls to reflect, to realign, and to live more purposefully. Like the Jaredites, I am faced with moments that call for faith over fear, humility over pride, and service over self-interest. And while these choices are not always easy, I am encouraged by the knowledge that they are part of a journey that stretches far beyond this moment. Every decision to choose kindness, to seek truth, to admit when I am wrong is a small step toward my own "promised land," a life that reflects the values I hold closest to my heart.

The Jaredite journey, with its lessons and its losses, leaves me with a sense of responsibility—not only to live these lessons but to share them in whatever ways I can. Just as Moroni preserved this story for future generations, I am reminded that the way I live, the choices I make, and the values I embody become part of a legacy, one that can uplift or dishearten those who come after me. Bearing witness to these truths is more than speaking or teaching; it is about letting my life itself be a testament to the power of faith, humility, and resilience.

As I move forward, I carry these pieces of wisdom with me, not as burdens but as guides. They remind me that the journey from Babel to Zarahemla is not about reaching a perfect state of enlightenment or achieving all my goals; it is about embracing a process of constant learning, growing, and realigning. In this way, the journey continues, and the wisdom I have gathered becomes a source of strength, helping me navigate the challenges and joys of life with a clearer sense of purpose.

In the end, I am deeply grateful for the Jaredite story and for the perspectives of other traditions that have enriched it. These lessons remind me that while I am but one part of a larger whole, my actions, my integrity, and my faith contribute to that whole in meaningful ways. The journey to Zarahemla is a personal one, but it is also a shared one, a journey that connects me to those who came before and to those who will follow. And with each step, I am reminded that no matter how far I may stray, there is always a way back, a way forward, and a way to guide me home.

Conclusion: From Babel to Zarahemla— The Journey to Our Promised Lands

Reflection on Babel and Zarahemla: Summarizing the Journey from Babel's Confusion to the Peace and Unity Represented by Zarahemla

As I reflect on the journey from Babel to Zarahemla, I see a movement that is not just about physical distance or ancient history—it is a journey that mirrors the path we all walk as we seek meaning, purpose, and connection in our lives. Babel, with its tower and its fractured tongues, stands as a symbol of human ambition, pride, and the consequences of striving without alignment to a higher purpose. Zarahemla, by contrast, represents a promised land—a place of unity, faith, and peace, grounded in humility and trust in God. The movement between these two points, from Babel's chaos to Zarahemla's harmony, is a journey that calls us to examine our own lives and to consider how we, too, can move from confusion toward clarity, from division toward unity, and from self-centered striving to purposeful living.

Babel's story is one of scattered intentions—a place where people sought to reach the heavens but lost their way in the pursuit. In Babel, we see the danger of pride and the pitfalls of seeking greatness without regard for others. The scattering of languages represents a loss of unity, a fracturing that happens when we elevate our own goals above those of our community, our values, and even our Creator. Babel stands as a reminder that ambition, when it ignores divine guidance and connection, often leaves us isolated, divided, and further from our true purpose. In Babel, I see not just a story of ancient people but a reflection of the times in my life when I have let pride, self-interest, or distraction distance me from my values and my deepest relationships.

Yet the journey does not end in Babel's confusion. The Jaredite journey takes us through trials and revelations, setbacks and transformations, guiding us toward Zarahemla—a place of peace, where people can find unity not through personal ambition but through shared purpose and humility. Zarahemla represents the peace that comes when we align ourselves with something greater than ourselves, when we prioritize relationships over ego, and when we seek connection with others and with God. It is a destination where individuals become a community, bound not by the desire to outdo one another but by the desire to lift one another up, to learn, to grow, and to journey together. Zarahemla is a place of "promised land" ideals, but it is also a state of being—a peace we find when our actions reflect our faith, our values, and our love for others.

The journey from Babel to Zarahemla is, then, both a metaphor and a guide. It invites us to reflect on the places in our own lives where we might still be in Babel, caught up in ambition, pride, or the illusion of self-sufficiency. It challenges us to consider how we might move toward Zarahemla, toward a life of connection, humility, and purpose. This path is not about achieving perfection; it is about being willing to realign, to listen, and to let our choices be guided by values that foster unity and peace rather than division and competition.

As I contemplate this journey, I am struck by how much it resonates with teachings from world religions and philosophies that emphasize the importance of unity, humility, and shared purpose. In Christianity, Jesus teaches, "Blessed are the peacemakers," reminding us that a life well-lived is one that seeks harmony and lifts others up. In Buddhism, the path to enlightenment involves releasing attachments and seeing beyond the self, embracing compassion as the foundation of peace. Islam teaches the value of humility and the beauty of community, emphasizing that we are stewards of one another, responsible for fostering kindness, justice, and unity. These teachings, woven through the journey from Babel to Zarahemla, remind me that the search for peace, purpose, and unity is a universal quest that transcends borders and beliefs.

In this sense, the journey from Babel to Zarahemla is both deeply personal and profoundly shared. Each of us, in our own way, is moving from our own forms of Babel—our moments of pride, isolation, or confusion—toward our own versions of Zarahemla, where we can find greater meaning, deeper connections, and lasting peace. This journey calls us to be patient with ourselves, to embrace humility, and to recognize that growth often happens through challenges. It teaches us that while confusion and division may sometimes feel inevitable, unity and peace are always within reach if we are willing to pursue them with integrity, faith, and an open heart.

The Jaredite story, with all its lessons and losses, has reminded me that Zarahemla is not a far-off ideal but a destination that becomes possible with each step we take toward living our values. In every act of kindness, every choice to seek understanding over judgment, every moment we choose humility over pride, we are moving closer to that promised land. As I close this reflection, I carry with me the knowledge that the journey from Babel to Zarahemla is a lifelong path, one that calls for persistence, patience, and a willingness to keep growing. And on that journey, I find a sense of peace, knowing that every step toward Zarahemla brings me closer to a life of purpose, unity, and the quiet strength that comes from living with integrity.

Connecting the Jaredite Journey to Modern Life: A Path from Confusion to Clarity, Humility, and Divine Connection

The Jaredite journey, from the scattered chaos of Babel to the promise of Zarahemla, resonates as more than an ancient tale; it mirrors the spiritual journey we each navigate today. The Jaredites' path from confusion to clarity, from pride to humility, and from isolation to divine connection speaks directly to our own lives, where we, too, are often caught between moments of doubt and the desire for something greater. Their journey shows us that the movement from Babel to Zarahemla is as relevant today as it was centuries ago, a timeless roadmap guiding us through the challenges, distractions, and breakthroughs of our own spiritual journeys.

Babel represents a state of disconnection—an ambition to reach great heights while losing sight of the unity and humility that keeps us grounded. In our modern world, Babel can be found in our tendency toward over-busyness, the pressures of achievement, and the distractions that pull us away from meaningful relationships and spiritual growth. Like the people of Babel, we may sometimes find ourselves striving in ways that leave us feeling scattered, confused, or distant from our core values. The Jaredites' decision to leave Babel was not just physical; it was a choice to seek a life with purpose and direction. Their journey reminds us that when we feel lost or overwhelmed, the first step is often an intentional shift in direction, a commitment to move from confusion toward clarity, from ego-driven goals toward a life aligned with our highest intentions.

Zarahemla, on the other hand, represents a destination of peace, unity, and divine connection. It symbolizes the "promised land" of our own lives—the state of being where we find harmony within ourselves and with those around us. But the journey to Zarahemla is not easy, nor is it straightforward. It requires humility, resilience, and a willingness to let go of pride, much like the Jaredites did as they built barges, faced the unknown, and relied on faith to light their way. The path to Zarahemla is a journey of continual realignment, one that calls us to set aside distractions, to quiet the noise of doubt, and to nurture a relationship with the divine. In a world that often rewards independence and self-sufficiency, the journey to Zarahemla reminds us that true peace comes not from going it alone but from embracing a sense of purpose and a deeper connection with God.

This Jaredite journey is echoed in the wisdom of world traditions. In Christianity, the path from Babel to Zarahemla resembles the journey of faith, moving from confusion and sin toward redemption and unity with God. In Buddhism, it mirrors the path of enlightenment—a movement from ignorance and attachment toward inner peace and compassion. Hinduism speaks to a similar journey through the concept of *moksha*, the soul's release from worldly confusion and the attainment of spiritual clarity and liberation. Islam, too, emphasizes the value of humility, with the faithful encouraged to submit to Allah's will, trusting that true peace is found in aligning with divine purpose rather than personal ambition. These teachings highlight a universal truth: that clarity, humility, and divine connection are the ultimate destinations of a well-lived life, guiding us toward a place where we find not only inner peace but also the strength to uplift others.

In our own lives, the journey from Babel to Zarahemla invites us to ask where we are on this path and where we might still be caught in the confusion of Babel. Are there areas where ambition or pride may be clouding our vision, where we may be striving for things that do not bring us closer to our purpose? Are there moments where doubt keeps us from trusting in a higher power or from relying on a strength beyond our own? The Jaredite journey calls us to pause, to reflect, and to choose a path that brings us closer to Zarahemla—a place of humility, connection, and alignment with divine guidance.

To live this journey means embracing faith as an active practice, one that shapes our decisions, our relationships, and our sense of self. It is about developing clarity through regular reflection, seeking not what is easiest or most convenient but what brings us closer to peace and purpose. It is about cultivating humility recognizing that true strength comes not from standing above others but from standing beside them, with compassion and understanding. And, ultimately, it is about fostering a connection with the divine, allowing God's light to illuminate the path forward, especially in times of uncertainty or darkness.

As we connect the Jaredite journey to our own lives, we find that each step from Babel to Zarahemla is a step toward becoming who we are truly meant to be. The journey reminds us that, even in moments of doubt or confusion, there is always a path back to clarity and peace. Through humility, we learn to let go of the need to control, to release the attachments that hold us back, and to trust that our journey, like the Jaredites, is guided by a purpose greater than ourselves. And as we walk this path, we find that Zarahemla is not only a destination—it is a way of being, a state of alignment with divine love, a place where our lives reflect the unity, peace, and joy that come from living with faith and intention.

The Jaredite journey teaches us that no matter how far we may wander, there is always a way back. Babel may be a familiar starting point, but Zarahemla is a destination we can reach, one step, one choice, one act of faith at a time. And as we walk this path, we create a life filled with purpose, integrity, and a quiet, unshakable peace— the very essence of the promised land that awaits each of us.

A Call to Seek Personal Promised Lands: Embracing a Journey of Faith, Integrity, and Divine Guidance

As we reflect on the Jaredite journey, we are reminded that each of us is on our own path toward a "promised land"—a place where faith, integrity, and divine guidance converge to bring us peace and purpose. For the Jaredites, the journey began with a willingness to leave behind the confusion of Babel and set out for something greater, something unknown. Like them, we are each called to seek our own promised lands, destinations that may be less about a physical place and more about a way of being—a life where we live in alignment with our values, find a deeper connection with God, and experience a sense of fulfillment and clarity. This journey is not easy, but it is a calling worth pursuing, one that invites us to become our truest selves, grounded in the principles that bring us closer to the divine.

The Jaredite story reveals that finding our promised land requires more than ambition or mere good intentions. It requires faith that pushes us beyond our comfort zones, a commitment to integrity that guides us even when the path is unclear, and a willingness to heed divine guidance, trusting that God's wisdom is greater than our own. In their journey, the Jaredites faced trials that tested their resolve, yet it was precisely in those moments that they grew—where their humility and resilience opened the way to new insights and where faith became their light. Their story serves as both a guide and a challenge, asking us if we, too, are willing to pursue our promised lands with the same courage, trust, and dedication.

This call to seek our promised lands is echoed in the teachings of many faiths. In Christianity, Jesus invites His followers to "seek first the kingdom of God" (Matthew 6:33), urging them to look beyond worldly concerns and prioritize their relationship with the divine. In Buddhism, the path to enlightenment is a journey that asks us to let go of attachments, to seek wisdom and compassion, and to embrace the peace that comes from aligning with truth. Islam emphasizes *tawakkul*, or reliance on God, encouraging believers to surrender their fears and desires to Allah, trusting in His guidance to lead them toward peace and fulfillment. And in Judaism, the journey to the "promised land" is both physical and spiritual, representing a return to the covenant and a life rooted in justice, compassion, and devotion.

Elder D. Todd Christofferson taught, "In the end, burying our weapons of rebellion leads to a unique joy. With all who have ever become converted to the Lord, we are 'brought to sing the song of redeeming love.'" The peace of a promised land is not found in avoiding mistakes but in embracing the journey of growth, allowing each misstep to teach us and each moment of grace to strengthen us. Each of these teachings invites us to look within, to examine our lives, and to pursue a path that brings us closer to the highest ideals of faith, integrity, and divine purpose.

To seek our promised lands, we must start by defining what they mean to us personally. What values and qualities do we want to cultivate? What kind of life do we hope to lead? The Jaredite journey shows us that a promised land is not just a goal but a reflection of who we are becoming along the way. It is a life lived with intentionality, where each step brings us closer to a deeper understanding of ourselves, of others, and of God. By focusing on the values that matter most—faith, humility, resilience, and compassion—we create a roadmap that guides us, even when the path seems unclear.

Here are some ways to actively pursue your own promised land of faith, integrity, and divine connection:

1. **Nurture a Spirit of Faith**: Like the brother of Jared, who sought divine guidance at every step, we are called to live by faith. This means choosing to trust in something greater than oneself, believing that each challenge can reveal something valuable. Spend time in prayer, meditation, or reflection, asking for guidance and listening for the quiet answers that may come. Faith is not a one-time choice but an ongoing journey, a daily decision to seek light, even in darkness.

2. **Live with Integrity**: Integrity is the foundation of any journey toward the promised land. Commit to aligning your actions with your values, even when it is difficult or inconvenient. Whether in your relationships, work, or personal growth, let honesty, kindness, and humility be your guide. Remember that integrity is built in small, consistent acts that gradually shape the person you are becoming.

3. **Embrace Humility and Openness**: The Jaredite story shows us that pride can become a barrier on the path to peace. Seek humility by recognizing that you do not have to have all the answers and that learning is a lifelong process. Be open to new perspectives, willing to change, and ready to let go of the things that no longer serve your growth. Humility allows us to move forward with clarity, accepting that we are part of a greater purpose.

4. **Practice Resilience through Challenges**: Just as the Jaredites faced storms and setbacks, we, too, will encounter challenges on our journey. Rather than seeing these as roadblocks, consider them as opportunities for growth. Reflect on past struggles that have strengthened your faith or shaped your character. Each obstacle you overcome brings you closer to the resilience needed to reach your own promised land.

5. **Seek Connection and Community**: The Jaredites were not alone on their journey, nor are we alone on our journey. Surround yourself with people who uplift and encourage you, who share your values and support your growth. Community can be a source of strength, offering guidance, encouragement, and accountability. By building connections with others, we create a shared journey where we lift each other up, moving closer to our promised lands together.

Ultimately, the call to seek our own promised lands is an invitation to a life of purpose, integrity, and faith. It is about becoming people who are led by higher principles, who are willing to step out of the familiar and into the unknown, trusting that each step forward brings us closer to the peace and fulfillment we seek. The journey from Babel to Zarahemla, from confusion to divine connection, is one we walk every day, in every choice we make and every value we uphold. And as we move forward, the teachings from the Jaredite story and from spiritual traditions around the world serve as our guiding lights, illuminating the path to the lives we hope to build.

So, may we each embrace this call to seek our personal promised lands with courage, faith, and open hearts. May we learn from the Jaredites' triumphs and trials, letting their wisdom inspire us to walk with purpose and resilience. And as we journey onward, may we find the peace, unity, and divine connection that await those who seek with sincerity and live with integrity. The promised land is not just a place; it is a way of being. And as we pursue it, we find that it is not only the destination but also the journey itself that transforms us, making each step one of discovery, growth, and grace.

APPENDIX: Reflection Themes Organized for Practical Use

Introduction

As we conclude this exploration of the Jaredite journey, we arrive at a collection of *Reflection Themes*—insights drawn from the Jaredites' story and enriched by wisdom from world traditions. These themes are more than philosophical ideas; they are practical guides for daily living, designed to help us connect with deeper values, strengthen our resilience, and enhance our relationships with others and with the divine. Each theme is an invitation to pause, reflect, and apply ancient wisdom to modern life, turning timeless lessons into transformative practices that support our spiritual growth.

This section organizes these themes for practical use, making it easier to apply them in moments of both triumph and trial. Each theme encourages self-reflection, offers prompts for intentional growth, and provides tools to build a life rooted in integrity, faith, and compassion. Whether you are seeking clarity in the midst of confusion, strength to endure a personal challenge, or inspiration to act with greater humility, these themes offer a starting point. They serve as reminders that the journey from confusion to connection, from doubt to divine guidance, is an ongoing process—one that unfolds with each choice, each reflection, and each act of faith.

Use these themes as touchstones, revisiting them whenever you need guidance, encouragement, or simply a moment to reconnect with your highest intentions. Like the journey of the Jaredites, our spiritual paths are filled with moments that call for courage, humility, and hope. These reflections are here to guide us along the way, helping us bring the wisdom of the past into our lives today, making each step one of purpose, growth, and meaning.

Building Faith and Personal Revelation: Seeking Divine Guidance

Faith and personal revelation are at the heart of a spiritually enriched life. They connect us to God, anchor us in purpose, and offer us a source of strength, comfort, and insight that grounds us in times of uncertainty. The journey of building faith and seeking revelation is about cultivating a relationship with the divine, where we listen, learn, and allow ourselves to be led. Across spiritual traditions—Judaism, Christianity, and Islam—faith and the pursuit of divine guidance are seen not only as acts of devotion but as daily practices that transform our lives.

Here is a guide to help you build faith and invite personal revelation, drawing on insights and practices from these faiths to strengthen your connection with God.

1. Prayer as a Path to Revelation ~ Prayer is the bridge between us and God—a channel for both expressing our needs and receiving divine insights. Through prayer, we open ourselves to guidance, inviting God to influence our lives and decisions. In each tradition, prayer is seen as both a sacred practice and a means of receiving revelation.

- **Judaism**: In Jewish tradition, *tefillah* (prayer) is a way to approach God with humility, acknowledging our dependence on His wisdom. The Amidah, a central prayer in Judaism, emphasizes gratitude, repentance, and requests for guidance. Jewish teachings remind us that prayer is not just about asking for things; it is about aligning ourselves with God's will and seeking to become vessels for divine purpose.

- **Christianity**: In Christianity, Jesus teaches, "Ask, and it will be given to you; seek, and you will find; knock, and it will be opened to you" (Matthew 7:7). This invitation to pray is not only about asking for blessings but about seeking a genuine connection with God. Through regular prayer and honest conversation with God, Christians believe they can receive personal revelation that illuminates their lives and leads them toward purpose.

- **Islam**: Prayer, or *salat*, is one of the Five Pillars of Islam and is seen as a way to submit to God's will, drawing closer to

His wisdom. Muslims pray five times a day, grounding their lives in moments of pause, reflection, and connection. Beyond formal prayer, *du'a*—personal supplication—is an open invitation for Muslims to ask God for guidance, seek forgiveness, and express gratitude. Through both *salat* and *du'a*, Muslims open their hearts to divine guidance and align their lives with God's path.

Practical Exercise ~ Create a prayer habit by setting aside time each day for intentional, open-hearted conversation with God. Be honest in your prayers, sharing your hopes and worries and seeking guidance. Approach prayer with gratitude and humility, allowing it to become a space where you listen as much as you speak.

2. Cultivating Faith Through Action ~ Faith is not just a feeling; it is an active commitment to live in trust, even when we cannot see the entire path ahead. Cultivating faith means practicing trust in God's wisdom and letting that trust guide our actions and decisions.

- **Judaism**: In Judaism, faith is often expressed through *emunah*, a Hebrew term that signifies trust in God's reliability. Faith is seen as something that grows through acts of kindness, justice, and commitment to God's commandments. Each action taken in line with *Emunah* deepens the believer's connection to God, creating a foundation of trust that sustains them.

- **Christianity**: The Epistle of James teaches, "Faith without works is dead" (James 2:26). For Christians, faith is brought to life through action—whether through acts of service, kindness, or integrity in daily life. Faith is more than a passive belief; it is a decision to act on God's promises and to live out His teachings in ways that serve others.

- **Islam**: In Islam, faith, or *iman*, is considered complete only when accompanied by action. Believers are called to engage in *amal salih* (righteous deeds), embodying their faith through acts of charity, honesty, and devotion to family and community. Faith in Islam, is strengthened as it is practiced, becoming an active choice to live with integrity and kindness.

Practical Exercise ~ Set a weekly intention to act on your faith. Choose one act of kindness, generosity, or service that allows you to live out your beliefs. Reflect on how these actions deepen your faith and bring you closer to divine purpose.

3. Listening for Divine Guidance ~ Personal revelation comes when we create space to listen, cultivating a posture of openness that invites God's insights and guidance into our lives. Across spiritual traditions, listening for divine guidance is seen as a form of humility, a willingness to receive rather than control.

- **Judaism**: The Jewish practice of studying Torah is more than an intellectual exercise; it is a spiritual act that invites divine insight. Jews believe that as they study scripture and reflect on its teachings, God reveals new understandings and guidance for their lives. Meditation on the words of the Torah becomes a way to attune to God's voice.

- **Christianity**: In Christianity, the Holy Spirit is often seen as the source of personal revelation, guiding believers in their thoughts, actions, and decisions. Christians are encouraged to "be still and know" (Psalm 46:10), creating moments of silence and reflection to hear God's voice. Through scripture study, meditation, and open-hearted listening, believers invite God's Spirit to illuminate their lives.

- **Islam**: In Islam, believers seek divine guidance by reciting and reflecting on the Quran, which Muslims consider to be the direct word of God. Muslims are encouraged to approach the Quran with humility, seeking *hikmah* (wisdom) in its teachings. Reflection on the Quran allows Muslims to find answers to their questions and direction in life, trusting that God will guide them on the straight path.

Practical Exercise ~ Dedicate time each day for stillness and reflection. Read a passage of scripture, a meaningful quote, or simply sit in silence, asking God to reveal His wisdom. Listen without expectation, allowing whatever insights come to guide your thoughts and actions.

4. Fostering a Spirit of Gratitude and Openness ~ A heart open to revelation is one that is also grounded in gratitude. Gratitude shifts our perspective, helping us recognize the blessings we already have and making us more receptive to divine guidance.

- **Judaism**. Jewish prayers often begin with blessings of gratitude, a practice that trains the mind to see God's presence in every part of life. The concept of *hakarat hatov*, or "recognizing the good," is a central tenet, encouraging believers to appreciate God's constant guidance and provision.

- **Christianity**: Paul's letter to the Thessalonians encourages believers to "give thanks in all circumstances" (1 Thessalonians 5:18). Gratitude in Christianity is a way of honoring God's presence and acknowledging His hand in all things. Practicing gratitude opens believers' hearts to receive God's love and direction more readily.

- **Islam**: In Islam, gratitude, or *shukr*, is both an act of worship and a pathway to closeness with God. Believers are taught to be grateful not only for blessings but also for challenges, trusting that everything is part of God's divine plan. Practicing gratitude aligns believers' hearts with God's will, fostering openness to His guidance.

Practical Exercise ~ Begin and end each day with a gratitude practice. Take a few moments to list things you are grateful for, noticing even the smallest blessings. This habit cultivates a spirit of openness, inviting God's presence and making space for personal revelation.

Embracing the Journey of Faith and Revelation

Building faith and inviting personal revelation is a journey, one that deepens over time through intentional practices, acts of kindness, and moments of openness. As you incorporate these principles into your life, let each practice become a step toward a greater connection with God. Remember that faith is not a static state; it is a dynamic relationship with the divine, one that grows with each prayer, each act of integrity, and each moment spent listening for God's guidance. As you embark on this journey, trust that divine insight will come, not always in the ways you expect but always in the ways you need, lighting your path and strengthening your spirit.

Leadership and Community Building: A Foundation of Integrity

True leadership is built on a foundation of integrity,—humility, gratitude, ethical decision-making, and a commitment to serving others. In a world that often equates leadership with power, authority, or self-promotion, it is refreshing to remember that the most impactful leaders are those who lead with humility, value transparency, and act with a genuine desire to uplift their communities. Integrity in leadership is not just about what leaders achieve; it is about how they achieve it and the positive legacy they leave behind in the lives they touch and the communities they strengthen. Drawing from the wisdom of Islam, Buddhism, and Latter-day Saint teachings, we find timeless principles that show us how to lead with integrity, fostering communities grounded in trust, resilience, and unity.

At the heart of integrity in leadership is humility, a trait that places the well-being of others above personal pride or ambition. Humble leaders recognize that their role is not to dominate but to serve to create an environment where others feel valued and heard. In Islam, the concept of *Khilafah*, or stewardship, teaches that leaders are caretakers, accountable to both their communities and to God for their actions. The Prophet Muhammad exemplified this by reminding his followers that "the leader of a people is their servant," emphasizing that true leadership is rooted in humility and compassion. Leaders are encouraged to approach their roles with gratitude, recognizing that leadership is a trust that comes with both privilege and responsibility.

Buddhism similarly emphasizes humility and selflessness in leadership, grounded in the concept of *dana*, or selfless giving. Buddhist teachings remind us that leaders should act not out of attachment to power but out of a desire to benefit others. In Buddhist communities, the ideal leader is often described as one who is free from ego, who practices *metta* (loving-kindness) and *karuna* (compassion), and who makes decisions based on the collective good rather than personal gain. Leadership, in this view, is an act of ethical service, requiring self-reflection, empathy, and a deep commitment to the well-being of others.

In Latter-day Saint teachings, integrity in leadership is tied closely to the principles of servant leadership and gratitude. Jesus Christ's example of washing His disciples' feet illustrates that true leadership is about service, about lifting others and putting their needs above one's own. This model of leadership teaches that greatness comes not from titles or recognition but from a heart willing to serve. LDS teachings encourage leaders to act with gratitude, to see their role as a blessing rather than a right, and to remain accountable to God and to those they lead. By approaching leadership with humility, gratitude, and integrity, leaders foster communities that are more unified, resilient, and faithful.

Building a community based on integrity and servant leadership requires a daily commitment to values that reinforce trust, honesty, and mutual support. Here are some practical ways to cultivate integrity in leadership and foster a culture of unity and ethical governance within communities:

1. Lead with Humility and Serve First ~ Effective leadership starts with humility, a recognition that the role of a leader is to serve rather than to be served. Leaders who lead with humility create a culture where others feel empowered and respected. Practice self-awareness by regularly reflecting on your motivations: Are you leading to elevate others or to elevate yourself? By prioritizing service over status, you foster trust and inspire others to contribute to the community in meaningful ways.

2. Cultivate Gratitude as a Foundation ~ Gratitude shifts our focus from personal ambition to appreciation for the opportunity to lead and serve. Regularly express gratitude to the team members, community, or organization you lead. Recognize the contributions of others and thank them for their efforts. Gratitude reminds us that leadership is a privilege, one that comes with the responsibility to act ethically and with care. A grateful heart is an anchor in times of challenge, helping leaders stay grounded and focused on the collective good.

3. Embrace Ethical Decision-Making ~ Integrity in leadership is sustained through ethical decision-making—choosing what is right over what is easy, beneficial, or convenient. Draw from the principle of *Khilafah* in Islam by viewing each decision as a trust, one that requires accountability to both God and the community. Take time to evaluate the impact of decisions on others and ensure that they align with core values of honesty, justice, and fairness. Ethical governance builds a legacy of trust and ensures that decisions benefit the whole, not just a select few.

4. Foster Open Communication and Transparency ~ Integrity is reinforced by transparency, by building open lines of communication that allow for feedback, collaboration, and mutual respect. Buddhist teachings encourage leaders to cultivate the *right speech*—to speak truthfully, kindly, and with clarity. In your role, prioritize honest communication, encourage feedback, and invite diverse perspectives. Transparency not only strengthens trust but also fosters a culture where community members feel safe to express concerns and ideas, promoting unity and collective progress.

5. Encourage Collaboration and Empowerment ~ Leaders with integrity do not seek to control; they seek to empower. Embrace the servant leadership model of Jesus Christ by helping others recognize and develop their strengths. Foster an environment where collaboration is valued over competition, where team members are encouraged to take initiative and are supported in their growth. A community that feels empowered and respected is more likely to be unified, resilient, and innovative, as members work together toward shared goals.

6. Engage in Regular Self-Reflection ~ The path of integrity requires continuous self-examination. Take time regularly to reflect on your role as a leader, to assess where you are succeeding and where you can improve. Islamic and Buddhist traditions both emphasize self-reflection as a means to cultivate humility and ethical behavior. Reflect on your impact, ask for feedback, and consider how you can better serve and uplift those you lead. Self-reflection keeps leaders grounded, ensuring that they remain aligned with their values and committed to ethical governance.

7. Practice Compassion and Empathy ~ At the heart of integrity in leadership is the ability to empathize with others. Compassionate leaders build stronger communities, as members feel valued and understood. Try to see situations from others' perspectives, to listen actively, and to respond with empathy. Compassion not only fosters unity but also creates a culture where challenges are approached collaboratively, where people feel safe and supported in facing adversity together.

8. Lead by Example, Inspire by Action ~ Integrity in leadership is ultimately demonstrated through action. Let your choices reflect the values you wish to see in your community. Uphold ethical standards, practice gratitude openly, and lead with a heart committed to service. By embodying these principles, you inspire others to follow suit, creating a ripple effect that strengthens the community as a whole.

As leaders, our actions shape the character of the communities we build. Integrity, humility, gratitude, and servant leadership are not only ideals to aspire to but practical tools that empower us to lead in ways that uplift and inspire others. Drawing on the insights from Islam, Buddhism, and LDS teachings, we find that true leadership is less about exerting control and more about creating a space for growth, unity, and trust. When we lead with integrity, we honor the people we serve, the values we uphold, and the legacy we leave behind.

By committing to these principles, we transform leadership from a position of authority into a vocation of service, fostering communities where individuals feel valued, connected, and inspired to contribute. Let us embrace the call to lead with integrity, to act with humility, and to build communities that reflect our highest ideals, becoming places of strength, compassion, and shared purpose. In doing so, we not only create lasting impact but also contribute to a world where leadership is defined not by power but by a commitment to the common good.

Cycles of Repentance and Redemption: Humility and Grace

Life is filled with moments where we stumble, fall, and find ourselves in need of a fresh start. The cycles of repentance and redemption are universal themes that teach us that every misstep holds the potential for growth, every setback a chance for renewal. In repentance, we confront our mistakes with honesty and humility, and in redemption, we embrace the grace that allows us to learn, heal, and move forward. From Christianity, Islam, Judaism, Hinduism, Buddhism, and Latter-day Saint teachings, we find perspectives on repentance that transcend time and culture, each one guiding us to a life of resilience, humility, and continuous growth.

In these cycles, repentance is not about dwelling on guilt but about realigning ourselves with truth and integrity. Redemption, in turn, is not a one-time event but an ongoing journey—a process that allows us to rise after each fall, stronger and wiser than before. These cycles remind us that growth is a continuous process and that divine grace is always available to lift us, no matter how many times we stumble.

Repentance as Transformation and Humility

In Christianity, repentance is central to the teachings of Jesus, who emphasized that turning away from sin and toward God is a path to inner peace and renewal. The parable of the Prodigal Son illustrates this beautifully: a young man who strays returns to his father in humility, seeking forgiveness, only to be welcomed with open arms. Here, repentance is not a punishment; it is a way back to love, to connection, and to grace. This cycle of repentance and redemption teaches us that humility is not a weakness but a strength, allowing us to see ourselves clearly and to reach for something higher. Christian teachings remind us that divine grace is not given sparingly but is always available for those willing to seek it.

In Islam, the concept of *tawbah*—or turning back to Allah—teaches that repentance is both an act of humility and a journey toward inner peace. The Quran encourages believers to seek forgiveness sincerely, reminding them that "Allah loves those who constantly turn to Him in repentance" (Quran 2:222). This perspective frames repentance as an act of resilience, a continual willingness to acknowledge mistakes and to strive for self-improvement. In Islam, repentance is about transformation, a process of realigning with the divine and purifying the heart. This cycle of returning to Allah is a reminder that humility and growth are inseparable, and that divine mercy awaits anyone willing to make the journey back.

Judaism, too, places a profound emphasis on *teshuvah*, or repentance, which means "returning." During the High Holy Days, Jewish believers engage in a process of self-examination, seeking to repair relationships and align their lives with God's will. Teshuvah is more than an apology; it is a commitment to change, to let go of old patterns, and to make amends wherever possible. The teachings of Judaism remind us that repentance is not simply about absolution but about becoming a better version of ourselves. Each cycle of teshuvah allows us to turn toward growth, forgiveness, and greater alignment with divine purpose.

Redemption as Continuous Growth and Divine Grace

In Hinduism, the concept of *karma* emphasizes that each action has a consequence, and yet, through acts of repentance, humility, and selfless service, we can overcome the limitations of our past choices. Hindu teachings emphasize that *moksha*, or liberation, comes not from avoiding mistakes but from learning and growing through them. By engaging in acts of compassion, self-awareness, and devotion, we can transform our lives, releasing old patterns and moving closer to spiritual freedom. Redemption, in Hinduism, is a process of gradual awakening, a journey of growth that is supported by the divine grace available to those who seek it sincerely.

In Buddhism, redemption is achieved through the cycle of *karma* and *samsara*—the understanding that our actions shape our experiences. While the path to enlightenment involves acknowledging mistakes and making amends, it also requires the cultivation of wisdom and compassion. Buddhism teaches that each act of mindfulness, kindness, and self-awareness breaks the cycle of suffering, allowing us to redeem our lives through conscious choices. In this way, redemption becomes a process of freeing ourselves from attachments and cultivating a peaceful mind. Each cycle of repentance—of recognizing mistakes and striving to improve—leads to a deeper sense of freedom and connection.

In Latter-day Saint teachings, repentance is a central part of spiritual growth, viewed as a gift that enables us to continually improve and align ourselves with God's will. The principle of repentance, when combined with the Savior's grace, is not only about avoiding sin but about becoming more Christlike with each step. This perspective emphasizes that redemption is available to all, regardless of how far one may have strayed. The Atonement of Jesus Christ is seen as the ultimate expression of divine grace, offering an endless opportunity for transformation and renewal. Each cycle of repentance brings us closer to our potential, reminding us that we are not defined by our mistakes but by our willingness to learn and grow from them.

Elder D Todd Christofferson captured this transformative process, reflecting on the example of the Anti-Nephi-Lehies: "Rather than risk any possible return to their prior state of rebellion against God, they buried their swords. And as they buried their physical weapons, with changed hearts, they also buried their disposition to sin." Repentance, like burying a weapon, is an act of letting go—not just of behavior but of the inner rebellion that keeps us from peace.

It invites us to trust in the transformative power of divine grace, which, as Elder Christofferson further teaches, "will forgive our sins and rebellions of the past and will take away the stain of those sins and rebellions from our hearts."

Embracing the Cycles of Repentance and Redemption in Our Own Lives

Repentance and redemption are not confined to moments of crisis; they are daily practices, ways of living that allow us to learn from each experience, to let go of what no longer serves us, and to move forward with renewed purpose. Here are some ways to embrace these cycles of growth, humility, and grace in everyday life:

1. **Reflect Honestly on Mistakes** ~ Each of us has moments where we fall short of our ideals. Take time regularly to reflect on your actions, being honest about where you may have strayed. By acknowledging our mistakes with humility,

we create space for growth and allow ourselves to realign ourselves with our values.

2. **Seek Forgiveness and Make Amends** ~ Repentance is not only a personal process but often involves reaching out to others. When possible, make amends with those you may have hurt, offering a sincere apology and seeking to repair any damage done. This act strengthens relationships, renews trust, and reflects a commitment to integrity.

3. **Learn and Move Forward** ~ True repentance involves a commitment to change. Reflect on what you can learn from each mistake, set specific intentions for how you can avoid similar missteps in the future. This approach allows you to transform regret into resilience, letting each experience guide you to better choices.

4. **Practice Self-Compassion** ~ Repentance and redemption require humility, but they also call for kindness toward oneself. Be patient with your growth, recognizing that perfection is not the goal. Each step, each effort, contributes to the process, and every attempt to improve brings you closer to your highest self.

5. **Embrace Grace and Let Go of Guilt** ~ Redemption is an invitation to leave guilt behind. Whether through prayer, meditation, or quiet reflection, find ways to release any

lingering feelings of unworthiness, embracing the grace that allows you to start anew. Trust that each cycle of repentance is part of a journey that brings you closer to the divine.

A Pathway to Lasting Change and Connection

The cycles of repentance and redemption remind us that we are not defined by our mistakes but by our willingness to learn, to grow, and to embrace the grace that allows us to become more than we once were. Whether through teshuvah, tawbah, or karma, the world's traditions show us that every misstep can be a steppingstone, each cycle a chance to become more compassionate, more mindful, and more aligned with our spiritual purpose.

As we embrace these cycles, we become resilient, learning to face life's challenges with humility and hope. Repentance is not about self-punishment; it is about transformation. Redemption is not a single moment but an unfolding process, a continuous journey of becoming. In each cycle, we find the opportunity to grow closer to God, to strengthen our character, and to build a life marked by resilience, integrity, and divine grace.

May we each find the courage to engage fully in the cycles of repentance and redemption, letting humility, growth, and grace shape our lives. And as we move through each cycle, may we draw closer to a life of purpose, peace, and profound connection with the divine.

Summary of Reflection Themes Organized for Practical Use

As we reach the conclusion of our *Reflection Themes*, we are reminded that true wisdom is not confined to the pages of history or bound to any single culture—it lives in our day-to-day choices, our relationships, and our inner journeys. These themes, gathered from the Jaredite story and enhanced by the teachings of world religions, offer us more than insights; they provide us with practical tools for personal growth, resilience, and connection. Whether we are seeking strength in the face of challenges, clarity in times of confusion, or a deeper sense of purpose, these reflections are here to guide us, grounding us in principles that transcend time and circumstance.

Each theme invites us to pause, reflect, and take intentional steps toward becoming our best selves. By exploring humility, resilience, integrity, and divine connection, we begin to craft a life rooted in values that not only enrich our own lives but uplift those around us. We find that these ancient principles are as relevant today as they were in the Jaredite journey, a reminder that the path to personal "promised lands" is paved with small, purposeful choices that align us with something greater than ourselves.

Let these reflection themes become part of your ongoing journey. Revisiting them as life presents new challenges and opportunities, allowing them to be steady companions, providing guidance, reassurance, and inspiration. In moments of uncertainty, let them remind you of your inner strength; in times of doubt, let them rekindle your faith; and in times of joy, let them deepen your gratitude.

Ultimately, these themes are more than reflections—they are invitations to live fully, to walk our paths with integrity, and to find peace in the journey. As you carry these insights forward, may they empower you to face each day with courage, clarity, and compassion, guiding you ever closer to a life of meaning, purpose, and divine connection.

References

Christianity

- Holy Bible. (2011). *New International Version*. Zondervan. (Original work published 1978)

- Lewis, C. S. (1952). *Mere Christianity*. HarperCollins.

- Wright, N. T. (2006). *Simply Christian: Why Christianity Makes Sense*. HarperOne.

Islam

- *The Quran* (M. A. S. Abdel Haleem, Trans.). (2004). Oxford University Press. (Original work published ca. 632)

- Nasr, S. H. (2002). *The Heart of Islam: Enduring Values for Humanity*. HarperOne.

- Esposito, J. L. (2011). *What Everyone Needs to Know About Islam* (2nd ed.). Oxford University Press.

Judaism

- The Jewish Publication Society. (1985). *Tanakh: The Holy Scriptures: The New JPS Translation According to the Traditional Hebrew Text*.

- Heschel, A. J. (1955). *God in Search of Man: A Philosophy of Judaism*. Farrar, Straus and Giroux.

- Wiesel, E. (1976). *Messengers of God: Biblical Portraits and Legends*. Random House.

Buddhism

- Dalai Lama. (2005). *The Universe in a Single Atom: The Convergence of Science and Spirituality*. Harmony Books.

- Rahula, W. (1959). *What the Buddha Taught* (Revised ed.). Grove Press.

- Thich Nhat Hanh. (1999). *The Heart of the Buddha's Teaching: Transforming Suffering into Peace, Joy, and Liberation*. Broadway Books.

Hinduism

- Easwaran, E. (Trans.). (2007). *The Bhagavad Gita* (2nd ed.). Nilgiri Press.

- Flood, G. (1996). *An Introduction to Hinduism*. Cambridge University Press.

- Radhakrishnan, S. (1948). *The Bhagavadgita: With an Introductory Essay, Sanskrit Text, English Translation, and Notes*. Harper & Brothers.

Latter-day Saint (LDS) Faith

- The Church of Jesus Christ of Latter-day Saints. (1981). *The Book of Mormon: Another Testament of Jesus Christ*. Salt Lake City, UT

- Christofferson, D. T. (2024, October). *Burying our weapons of rebellion*. General Conference of The Church of Jesus Christ of Latter-day Saints. Salt Lake City, UT. https://www.churchofjesuschrist.org

- Hinckley, G. B. (2000). *Standing for Something: 10 Neglected Virtues That Will Heal Our Hearts and Homes.* Three Rivers Press.

- Benson, E. T. (1989, April). *Beware of pride.* General Conference of The Church of Jesus Christ of Latter-day Saints. Salt Lake City, UT. https://www.churchofjesuschrist.org

- Nibley, H. W. (1988). *The World and the Prophets.* Deseret Book Company.